Tides of Consent

How Public Opinion Shapes American Politics

Politics is a trial in which those in government – and those who aspire to serve – make proposals, debate alternatives, and pass laws. Then the jury of public opinion decides. It likes the proposals or actions or it does not. It trusts the actors or it doesn't. It moves, always at the margin, and then those who benefit from the movement are declared winners. This book is about that public opinion response. Its most basic premise is that although public opinion rarely matters in a democracy, public opinion change is the exception. Public opinion rarely matters, because the public rarely cares enough to act on its concerns or preferences. Change happens only when the threshold of normal public inattention is crossed. When public opinion changes, governments rise or fall, elections are won or lost, and old realities give way to new demands.

James A. Stimson is the Raymond Dawson Distinguished Bicentennial Professor of Political Science at the University of North Carolina at Chapel Hill. He is a former president of the Midwest Political Science Association and treasurer of the American Political Science Association. He has authored and coauthored numerous books, including *Yeas and Nays: Normal Decision-Making in the U.S. House of Representatives*, *Issue Evolution: Race and the Reconstruction of American Politics*, *Public Opinion in America*, and *The Macro Polity*. Professor Stimson has served as editor of *Political Analysis* and has served on the editorial boards of journals such as the *American Journal of Political Science* and the *Journal of Politics*. He is the author of many articles published in major journals of political science and is the recipient of various awards for his distinguished scholarship.

Tides of Consent

How Public Opinion Shapes American Politics

JAMES A. STIMSON
University of North Carolina

CAMBRIDGE
UNIVERSITY PRESS

HN
90
.P8
S845
2004

CAMBRIDGE UNIVERSITY PRESS
Cambridge, New York, Melbourne, Madrid, Cape Town, Singapore, São Paulo

Cambridge University Press
40 West 20th Street, New York, NY 10011–4211, USA
www.cambridge.org
Information on this title:www.cambridge.org/9780521841344

First published 2004
Reprinted 2005

Printed in the United States of America

A catalogue record for this book is available from the British Library.

Library of Congress Cataloging in Publication Data
Stimson, James A.
Tides of consent : how opinion movements shape American politics / James A. Stimson.
    p.   cm.
Includes bibliographical references and index.
ISBN 0-521-84134-8 – ISBN 0-521-60117-7(pb.)
1. Public opinion – United States.   2. United States – Politics and government – Public
opinion.   I. Title.
HN90.P8S45   2004
    320.973–dc22   2004045107

ISBN-13   978-0-521-84134-4 hardback
ISBN-10   0-521-484134-8 hardback

ISBN-13   978-0-521-60117-7 paperback
ISBN-10   0-521-60117-7 paperback

To Bill Flanigan, Frank Sorauf, Don Matthews, and Ray Dawson.
In recognition of old debts, never repaid.

Contents

List of Tables and Figures

TABLES

FIGURES

Preface

The Shutdown

Bill Clinton was repudiated. The 1994 congressional elections, a triumph for the Republicans and their "Contract with America," left newly elevated House Speaker Newt Gingrich in charge, proclaiming the president of the United States "irrelevant." What ensued, in two stages, was a rare attempt at congressional government, at setting the public agenda from Capitol Hill. The first stage was the "contract," a series of carefully staged votes in the first 100 days of the new Congress. Nine of ten items passed, some surprisingly easily, although the Republican Senate, less enthusiastic by far, was slow to follow up and Bill Clinton stood ready to veto most of what did get Senate approval.

The second stage, unlike the first, was not raised for public debate during the elections. It was an attempt to alter fundamentally the shape of the federal budget. With the enthusiasm born of being newly in control, Gingrich and the Republicans set out to achieve the goal that had always eluded Republicans, that had eluded even Ronald Reagan: to cut down on scale of government in the domestic sphere.[1] They would pass a budget that would zero out spending programs (for example, the Corporation for Public Broadcasting) and that would actually reduce spending across the board for health care, education, environment, and welfare. Cutting welfare was popular, had always been. But when Gingrich opined that orphanages weren't such a bad way to deal with dependent children, the public was reminded that welfare cuts might not be costless.

---

[1] Reagan, in 1981, had succeeded in cutting the growth of domestic spending, reining in increases, but had not achieved actual cuts. In later budgets he could not even slow the momentum.

But for this crucial second stage there was a problem: The president was not in fact irrelevant. No spending bill could become law without his signature or a two-thirds' vote to override his veto. He predictably would not sign. And the bills, as if stamped "Made by the Republican Party," had no chance of achieving the Democratic votes that would be required for override. The well-worn path for such deadlocks is compromise. When either side can block but neither can pass its preferences into law, meeting somewhere close to the middle is the winning solution that emerges. But the election had been billed a "Republican Revolution," and its winners, believing the wind of public support was at their backs, were thinking like revolutionaries. And so they decided to gamble. Gingrich announced early in the process that there would be no compromise, that the Republican Congress would write a Republican budget and send it to the president with two choices: Sign it or shut down the government when the fiscal year expired with no budget.

The Congress, after passing almost all of the "contract" items in the first 100 days, as promised, was popular as never before. Gingrich promised, Gingrich delivered, and Speaker Gingrich was in the driver's seat. Congress, never popular with the American public, was drawing an approval of 47 percent. With the public behind him and an unpopular president with a history of backing down when challenged, this aggressive strategy seemed as though it could work. The mechanism to implement Gingrich's plan was simple. Not passing the budget before the beginning of the fiscal year was far from unusual; in more years than not some of the appropriations were not yet law with the onset of the new budget year. Congress historically has coped with such situations by using "continuing resolutions," a device that allowed the government to continue operating as it did under the expired budget. This time there would be no continuing resolution.[2] President Clinton could sign on to the Republican plan or watch government halt, waiting until the cumulated injury and inconvenience forced him to capitulate.

Public opinion would arbitrate the conflict. If Clinton showed reluctance to accommodate, then an angry electorate would push him to do so. That was the operating theory in April and May when the strategy was put into place. The public, however, thought it was a bluff, that

---

[2] The Republican Congress actually did pass continuing resolutions (several in the end), one to put off the deadlock until mid-November and then another with "poison pill" provisions that were calculated to force a presidential veto, a shrewd tactic designed to make the presidential action appear to precipitate the crisis. It did not help the Republican cause that one of those poison pills was a very unpopular increase in Medicare premiums.

the showdown would not come to pass. By 77 percent and 79 percent, respectively, NBC News and *Wall Street Journal* polls of September and October predicted that the budget would be resolved somehow without a shutdown. Threatening dire consequences is a fairly normal part of hard bargaining. It had been done before. But Gingrich and the Republicans might have been made nervous by an October poll that showed that more Americans would blame Congress (43%) than the president (32%) if the shutdown did come to pass. Since the heady days of spring, Congress had gone beyond the popular "contract" items into new territory, such as defunding public television and threatening many popular domestic programs. The "contract" had been billed as "reform." The steps beyond, far less popular, were attacks on programs and values that enjoyed wide public support. While Congress was losing public esteem, the president gained a little, moving from approval in the mid-40s during Gingrich's first 100 days to low 50s by the time of the showdown in November. Perhaps a more popular president facing a less popular Congress might not back down after all.

The media, like the public, generally regarded the shutdown as a political bluff. Stories of the dislocations to come emphasized the inessential, cosmetic side of government. Families vacationing in the capital might not be able to visit some national monuments, perhaps not see the wildlife in Western parks. There was no sense of crisis, that anything that really mattered might be seriously affected.

That was not to be the case. When the government actually shut down, partial though the shutdown was, the effects were anything but cosmetic. About 800,000 federal employees were forced to stay home without pay.[3] "Bureaucrats" have never been popular, but these people turned out to be just ordinary people who worked for a living and had mortgages to pay. Hundreds of employers who performed a myriad of contractual services for government and the public immediately shut down and laid off their workers. Much of the government, we quickly learned, was not really government. It was private firms paid by government serving government needs. Unlike the federal employees, where one could at least imagine that an eventual settlement might compensate lost pay, the private sector employees furloughed by the shutdown were innocent victims for whom there would be no compensation. The shutdown was not just

---

[3] White House staffers were among those furloughed. Interns were called on to cover staff functions. That brought the president together with one Monica Lewinsky, the result of which is history.

about aborted vacation plans; it was about lives disrupted. A Gallup survey soon after the onset captured a concerned public. Asked whether the partial shutdown was a serious problem, 51 percent said that it was a crisis or a serious problem. Only 14 percent said it was not a problem. People who thought government played little role in their daily lives discovered by the shock of its absence that it did. And the dimensions were more than personal. Wall Street and the financial community were distressed to learn that the thousands of people who labored to collect economic statistics, the raw numbers that are the basis for all planning and forecasting of economic trends, were off the job, not collecting the data. The numbers would still flow, but the lost work days put into question whether they could be believed.

If Republicans were troubled by early polls that speculated on who might be blamed, after the shutdown began came polls that were no longer speculations. The public was much more inclined to blame "Republican leaders in Congress" (49%) than the president (26%), with another 20 percent or so condemning both equally. All of a sudden it was becoming clear that the pressure to compromise would not be on Clinton alone. The shutdown wasn't a mere bargaining game. The public was angry, and someone was going to pay in lost political standing. Public inattention to politics is legendary. But 80 percent of all Americans reported paying close attention to the shutdown in a January survey by Pew. It was a crisis. It would have consequences.

The consequences were felt in Congress. From the April high point of 47 percent, congressional approval had fallen steadily, not just back to its normal level of about 36 percent, but below that, down to the low 20s during the November shutdown. "Approval of Congress" is something that leaders feel very directly; its import is that it mirrors their own personal standing and, with the Congress so clearly identified with one party, the party's standing too. Meanwhile, Bill Clinton's public standing improved. The crisis perhaps did not benefit the president; it clearly did not hurt him. The pressure to settle now shifted. Clinton looked as if he could hold out indefinitely. The Republican congressional leadership could not.

More than others, Bob Dole, Senate majority leader and candidate to oppose Bill Clinton in 1996 for the presidency, was feeling the heat. Early soundings suggested that the shutdown was harming Republican prospects for 1996 and was tying Dole in the public mind to an increasingly unpopular Gingrich. Republicans relented and came to terms on a temporary deal to keep the government operating another month.

When the government shut down again in mid-December, there was no longer any suspense about who was winning and losing the tug of war. Dole's presidential campaign had suffered damage from which it would not recover. Clinton was hanging tough for the first time in his presidency and enjoying public support for doing so. As the pain of public rejection began to be felt, Republican unity began to fold. Dole's Senate Republicans began working a deal with the White House amid talk of sell-out from the House freshmen, who saw their balanced budget plan and the shutdown as a historic mission.

The Republicans had wanted to wage a war of principle over balancing the federal budget in seven years.[4] Their plan proposed some hard and serious medicine, severe cuts to the Medicare and Medicaid programs whose rapid growth had much to do with the budget numbers. The weakness in their bargaining position was that the money saved on the popular health programs was about the same amount as their proposed new tax cut. It was not painful medicine for balancing the budget, it was seen as painful medicine to finance a tax cut, sacrificing the poor and the elderly for a break to high-income taxpayers. That was not a winnable position.

With Dole moving toward settlement and the House freshmen out ahead of Gingrich girding for combat, the *New York Times*'s headline of January 5, 1996, captured the feeling: "Battle over the Budget: The Republicans; Split and Bruised in Polls, G.O.P. Weighs New Tactics." Now it was a salvage operation. The nation had decided. The Republicans had lost their high-stakes bid. When they passed yet another continuing resolution in January, the extension was still temporary, and there was talk of yet another shutdown to come. But the talk was face-saving. There would not be another shutdown. The Republican Congress had fallen so far so fast that instead of further conflict with Bill Clinton, Republican leadership in both houses began looking for Clinton measures they might pass before the election in order to repair their image of uncompromising revolutionaries.

This story, and many like it, shows the dominating role of opinion movements. The game in Washington is played to win the game in the country. The issue is not the "polls," a term by which we disparage public opinion. The polls are measuring devices. It is not the numbers; it is what

---

[4] The irony in this story is striking. Having staked all on a plan to balance the budget in seven years (by fiscal 2002), a plan thought at the time to be too ambitious to succeed, the surging economy of the 1990s (and the 1993 increased tax rates) did in three years what the lost plan could not do in seven.

they mean. It is the real movements by the national electorate that the polls measure that move politics.

Public opinion matters. It moves in meaningful ways, the players in Washington attend closely, and the public governs, much more than most realize. Its power is the inertia. Once in motion, it can no more be reversed than can the tides be halted. Something sets it in motion and it creeps, as the tides come in, steadily toward a new position. Its power is that it points always to the future, telling those whose careers and strategies depend on public support that success depends on being with the tide, not against it.

It is probably impossible to say what single thing is the most important factor in American politics, but I believe that thing is public opinion movement. I believe that it is the drive wheel. And important though it is, we have only scratched the surface of understanding opinion movement. It is almost unknown in a systematic sense, in a sense of regular theories and analyses. But commentary about opinion movement is ubiquitous. Take away the sense that opinion is shifting and the thoughts of many political analysts would lose their motivating force.

Tracing movements and showing consequences is the central theme of this book. Its claim is that change over time is what moves politics. Its design is to look at change over time in many different facets of public preferences, behavior, and response. It looks at movements on a time scale as fine as day to day and at movements that run a decade to completion. It is a story of American politics that will seem familiar in many regards, but one that puts the public in the driver's seat of politics, a common view of how democracy should be, a quite uncommon view of how it is.

Elections matter ultimately, because they force politicians to worry about the future, to attend to the present with a very sharp eye. But most of the effects that matter don't happen in elections. Politics is fast moving; it can't wait for a referendum scheduled months or years in the future. Our view of a gentle, slow-moving sequence in which citizens form opinions, express them at the polls, and then get a response from government – a product of political theory more than observation – doesn't come to terms with highly ambitious players in the political game, players who understand that they must anticipate where movement is heading before it gets there, that they must act now because later is too late.

But this isn't public opinion as commonly understood, that is, which percent favors or opposes some proposal, approves or disapproves of the president. *It is movement that matters*. Politicians ask, "How will the public respond?" and watch change for the answer. We have long known and noted a disconnect between many of the things citizens say they want and what government does. This static opinion is often toothless. When politicians know that the important public consensus is on lack of real concern about an issue, then the fact that what government does violates what citizens say they want will occur routinely. What citizens really want in these cases is not to pay attention, not to have concern about government intrusion into their lives. And that they get.

But opinion movement is a different story altogether. When public opinion changes, then the slumbering bear is alive; something has wakened it and it is wise to watch where it will go and what it will do. *Change happens when people care.* When people care, it is most unwise to stand against it. It is one of the tougher tricks in politics to know when the public does not care, when its apparent view can be ignored because it doesn't want to be bothered, and when it is aroused, in which case the rules change.

Movement in opinion often seems jerky and incoherent. Support for some positions goes up by a point or two, back down a little, up again, and so on. That is only on the surface. When we get beneath it to the public itself, not just the samples of it, it is a smooth path from here to there like that of a giant ship, not jerky like a kite. We don't often see that, because it requires a large amount of data and a belief in the smoothness to go after it. But that is what matters and that is what we see in this book.

ON POINT OF VIEW

This view is contrary to most (but not all) of what is written about public opinion in scholarly studies, contrary to a thirty-second-ad approach to politics, contrary to much that is reported as news. Coming to terms with the contradictions requires thinking about individuals and aggregates and requires looking at a lot of evidence. That is what this book is all about.

We have begun, in recent years, to think about public opinion in the aggregate – whole electorates rather than individuals. And we have begun to think about how those aggregates move over time. This new science of public opinion is almost wholly different from everything that went before. It differs decisively in finding order and pattern in how electorates respond to politics. Some of this new work is my own. It allows me to tell a story about how ordinary people engage in politics.

Much of that story is already written, although some is new. It fills scholarly journals with equations and analyses. But one of the beauties of this style of thinking is that it appeals to the native good sense of ordinary readers. It does not need equations. Its analyses can be expressed in simple English. My intention here is nothing less than to write a complete story of public opinion and to write it for readers who may know a little about politics but nothing about equations and regressions, nothing about the jargon of public opinion research.

ON HOW THE BOOK CAME TO BE WRITTEN

From the late 1980s I have been working on opinion dynamics, exploring how opinions move in the aggregate over time, why, and with what consequence for politics. From the beginning it was clear that these topics are of interest to people who care about politics and public affairs. Unlike most work on public opinion, which focuses on individual psychology and has no direct application to practical politics, opinion movement immediately strikes most people as exactly what they want to know to understand politics. In a word, it is intuitive.

In my first book on the topic, *Public Opinion in America* (Stimson 1991), I was torn between two writing goals: telling a story for general readers about how opinions move politics in America and convincing the scholarly community that the theory, concepts, and technology I had developed had a place in understanding public opinion. Ultimately, I concluded that no compromise was possible, that the book had to be either one or the other but could not be both. I chose to write a scholarly book, introducing the concept of public mood and the technology for estimating it. (This is some of the materials of Chapters 2 and 3.) The book was successful, but I was disappointed that the heavy-duty scholarship made it inaccessible to all but public opinion professionals. So, part of this book is a return to that lost goal, writing about what we know about public opinion movement for an audience that cares about politics.

During election year 2000 I decided on an effort, half work and half play, to track the presidential campaign on a daily basis. I wanted to study the campaign, and particularly the horse-race polling, as it happened, day by day. I wanted to see freshly what happened and what mattered, without the prejudice of looking back and knowing how it turned out. The technology that I had developed allowed me to take all the polls, as they were published, and solve for the standing of the candidates. This was an improvement over the public debate on polls, which observed that they differed a bit and argued, endlessly, about which of them should be believed. Using all of them is undeniably better than any one.[5] I posted my daily estimates to a Web site just for the fun of it. Trying to figure out what it all meant while it was going on led me to conclude that we don't know much at all about presidential campaign dynamics. That is the origin of the analyses of Chapter 4.

Earlier that year I had conducted a graduate seminar at the University of North Carolina at Chapel Hill on the topic of macro theory and research. It was a wonderful experience (and not all seminars are) and left me impressed both with how much we had learned in a brief time and with how little of this knowledge was working its way back inside the Beltway, where politics is practiced. My own research program at the time is now published (Erikson, MacKuen, and Stimson 2002) and many of those student papers are making their way into scholarly journals. Among the set of graduate student papers, three of them left an imprint on my Chapter 5. These were works on "Trust in Government" (Luke Keele), approval of Congress (Adam Newmark), and U.S. Senator approval (Jennifer Anderson).[6]

These influences come together in this book. Most important is my desire to take what we know and make it accessible, without the tedious detail that haunts survey research and without the jargon and technology of the dynamics approach. My thought when I began to observe opinion movements was that this was just what my intuition had always said public opinion should be. I hope readers will see it as I do.

ON TRUTH, OBJECTIVITY, AND SPIN

Much writing about public opinion is adversarial. It takes a view, from left or right, and proceeds to construct a set of facts that supports the view. It is spin. That kind of thing, call it rhetoric, is how politics works. It is part of the process.

There is nothing wrong with that, except that once you have figured out the perspective, it becomes predictable, and what is predictable is

---

[5] Because news organizations commission polls (thank goodness), they naturally report on their own product. The effect of this is that on a typical day, five organizations might be writing stories about their tracking polls of 800 respondents, each of which has a *lot* of sampling fluctuation. The total of all five is like a sample of 4,000, very reliable. Because no one owns it, this much better estimate goes unreported.

[6] The Anderson and Newmark research was later combined and published (Anderson and Newmark 2002).

boring. Telling the story objectively, just trying to get it right, is much more challenging. Objectivity of all kinds is difficult. In politics it is more difficult still. But the reward is great. It promises to convey truth, the real thing, not truths that can all be set aside by dismissing the prejudices that produced the perspective.

Critics of this more scientific approach to knowledge tell us that objectivity is impossible. And they are correct; it is. But the goal of objectivity is not. And if it is unobtainable, that does not make it less worthy. What I can say about the views I bring to understanding public opinion is that objective truth is my goal. Objectivity is the standard by which I wish to be judged. And when I fall short of meeting the standard, it is from my limitations of knowledge and vision, not from intent.

Acknowledgments

Although written in 2002 and 2003, this book has a history. Its contents reflect a good deal of the joint product of seventeen years of active collaboration with Robert S. Erikson and Michael B. MacKuen. When ideas are shared, as many in this book have been, they become melded by all and lose most of their original authorship. So it is true to say that of the many ideas we have shared, many of which are in this book, it is no longer clear where most originated and what they would have been if not critiqued and revised by the interchange of coauthorship. Mike and Bob have not joined in authoring this book, but I am sure they will find much of themselves in it. It is trite, but necessary, to say that I am alone responsible for errors of fact or interpretation.

I owe a special debt to John McIver. John read the manuscript with care, commented at great length and detail, and improved the book in hundreds of matters, some large. Many coauthors have done less to shape a final product. Paul Kellstedt, Dianne Stimson, and one anonymous referee for Cambridge University Press have also read the manuscript in full and pressed me to do better on many fronts. Daniel Hamilton read the manuscript with a focus on accessibility issues and pointed out problems that required better writing.

Lucy Bryan, James Campbell, Chris Ellis, Larry Grossback, Chuck Myers, David Peterson, Joe Ura, and Chris Wlezien have read and commented on portions of the book. The issue evolution theory of Chapter 3 was developed jointly with Edward G. Carmines. The ideas in Chapter 6 on the emergent properties of aggregates in a population of mixed political response styles were sharpened by highly focused discussions on information processing and aggregation with Jorge Bravo, Evan Parker-Stephen, and Ashleigh Smith. Students in my honors sections of the Introduction to American Government in 2002 and 2003 have read the manuscript and helped it by pointing out problems with accessibility. Larry Dodd is owed a special thanks for encouraging an earlier book that lent much to this effort.

Although well hidden in this work, the raw data archived by the Roper Center for Public Opinion Research of the University of Connecticut at Storrs are what make possible the serious study of public opinion change. I am grateful to the director, Richard Rockwell, and to Lois Timms-Ferrara, Marc Maynard, and Marilyn Milliken for generous assistance in my efforts. Portions of Chapter 1 and virtually all of Chapter 5 rely on the Job Approval Ratings database of state polls, a cooperative project of the University of Rochester, the University of North Carolina at Chapel Hill, and George Washington University, a wonderful contribution to opinion scholarship of Richard Niemi, Thad Beyle, and Lee Sigelman.

And finally, I thank the members of the American Politics Research Group of the University of North Carolina at Chapel Hill. That remarkable assemblage is where all my ideas are first tested, and where the worst ones are put to rest.

Tides of Consent
How Public Opinion Shapes American Politics

Opinion Flows

It came down to the hostages. On the evening of November 3, 1980, hoping to win another term in the White House, Jimmy Carter was trailing in the polls. Only days before, they showed him dead even with Ronald Reagan. Now they showed a trend toward Reagan. While the public polls showed either a small Reagan lead or a dead heat, Carter knew better. He knew that Reagan led and that the lead was growing. A few days earlier, coming on the heels of a media "celebration" of the first year of captivity of American hostages in Iran, the Iranians had announced harsh new conditions for a negotiated hostage release. The Iranians understood that they had a card to play in the pressure on Carter to achieve progress before election day. Now they had played it skillfully. Deeply embarrassed by his – and the nation's – impotence in the face of the Iranian clerics, Carter had seen his standing plummet over the hostage issue. He had tried diplomacy, and it had not worked. He had fashioned a military raid, and men had died, achieving nothing.

On Sunday, after the Iranian announcement, Carter's pollster Pat Caddell had Reagan leading by five points. On Monday evening, election eve, a new Caddell poll put the lead at ten. It was given to Carter on Air Force One en route to his Georgia home for election day. "That's when, frankly, we knew the gig was totally up," Caddell said (*New York Times*, November 5, 1980). Casting his vote in Plains, Georgia, the next day, Carter failed to put forward the expected election day optimism. As if preparing in advance for a concession speech to come, he talked to his townspeople about difficult political decisions in his administration.

Election day confirmed the trend toward Reagan. He would win and by a much bigger margin than anyone thought. The trend was real. As if to get it over and stanch the pain, Carter conceded early. He congratulated Reagan at 9:50 Eastern time, over an hour before the polls would close on the West Coast, a decision that might have turned some close races against now embittered Democratic candidates. He had wanted to do so an hour earlier, when desperate staff members did what they could to stall his desire to have it over. The campaign, it was clear, ended Monday evening on Air Force One.

We write a good deal about campaigns, the focus on who wins, who loses, and why. I want to ask a different question: Where do trends come from? Why is it that candidates surge ahead or fall behind? But that is only part of the issue. Had Jimmy Carter been, say, eleven points ahead – not unusual for a president seeking a second term – then a ten-point Reagan surge would have been a mere footnote to electoral history. So we need to think of trends of another sort and ask why this election, which should not have been close under normal circumstances, was close enough that last-minute events a world away could tip it. What was going on in the Carter presidency that made Carter vulnerable at the last? Why was Carter's standing so low? That question would force us to notice, for example, an election-year recession as the sort of thing that could make an incumbent president vulnerable.

Trends that had been in motion long before election year 1980 began also are part of the story. The stage began to be set early in the 1970s when Americans started thinking that they did not like many of the big government programs that had been popular when enacted. They began to think differently and began to want a different kind of leadership. All this was in place before Ronald Reagan became a candidate; indeed, it helps to explain why he and not someone else, someone more moderate, became the Republican candidate. Setting aside hostages and recessions, we need to understand how the profoundly conservative Ronald Reagan could have captured a nomination and how he could be a serious contender for the presidency. That will require us to understand the dynamics of public preference, why it is that the American public changes what it wants or doesn't want from government. These changes are glacial in pace as compared with even the month-to-month effects of economics, let alone the daily advances and declines of campaign momentum. The conservatism that heralded Ronald Reagan into the White House had been building for most of a decade. It had nothing at all to do with a 1979 hostage taking or a 1980 recession.

Politicians act on the public stage and the public responds. It is like a sport in which the judging comes after. But it does not come immediately after. Some of it comes quickly, in days. Some takes weeks and months. Some takes longer still. The ebb and flow of public response is going on always, but more intensely during the peak of campaign season when attention is focused on politics. These processes, taken together, fundamentally shape what politics means. They set parameters on what government can do, on what political pitches will work, what ones won't. A crusade against government at most times and places would fall flat, would be a losing strategy. In the fall of 1980 it was a winner for Ronald Reagan. That is the class of processes that needs explanation. What flows are under way at what times? What starts them? How do they flow? How far does the tide run before it ebbs and runs back again?

We vote for president on one day every four years. If we could hold the contest over and over again, would it always come out the same? The 1980 case, a quite decisive win for Reagan, might have come out differently in October than it did in November – or perhaps in December. If it had been held in November 1979, the polls suggest that it would have ended in an easy win for Carter. That gives some perspective to interpretations that have the character of claiming that outcomes were inevitable, that one candidate won because he was the right candidate with the right message, running a good campaign. To all those we need to add, "at the right time." Because we now know that public opinion is in flux.

The knowledge that public opinion moves gives us new power to understand American politics. We can take a familiar question, such as explaining the 1980 outcome, and answer it in the context of time and flow. What was happening day by day? What were the longer term flows on which these day-by-day movements were built? It is like waves. We understand that they move up and down. But we also understand that the up and down occurs along with larger movements, the tides. We need to understand both.

When analysts sit down to explain elections after the fact, there are three common stories. One is the campaign. If only some last-minute events, for example, the Iranian statement, had been different, the final days might have drifted in a different direction. Others focus on elections as referenda on the competence of the incumbent. In this story, Carter's problem was not the pre-election events, it was the year of inability to deal with hostages and economic misery that came before. Those who believe that elections register public choice about the direction government should pursue would have a different take altogether. What the 1980 presidential election was about, they would say, was a fundamental choice between liberal and conservative government. Voters in that year, reacting to a perception that government had grown large and ineffective, wanted the conservative alternative. If Americans had not been drifting toward conservatism, they would say, Carter would not have needed approval or favorable events to succeed in the routine business of winning a second term.

Analysts usually adopt one of these stories and assert that it is the real account of an election. Each is plausible, offered alone. The data speak to all three and say yes, that could be the way it was. Which story is true? All have been told. All stories have theories that claim them to be the explanation. But the reality is that it takes all three. Politics is dynamic on multiple scales. Policy preferences move over decades. Approval can change substantially within a single year – and it did in 1980. And the campaign has a daily dynamic, as themes are tried out and some work, some don't.

SEPTEMBER 11, 2001

Rudy Giuliani was a troubled mayor. His run for the Senate was aborted by the one-two punch of a nasty impending divorce and health problems. He had been tossed out of his home, which was awkward, because his home was Gracie Mansion, New York City's official mayoral residence. And then came September 11. The World Trade Center terrorism presented Giuliani with an extraordinary challenge. His city was in crisis, the likes of which it had never seen. Giuliani stepped to the fore and engaged in some of the most extraordinary political leadership of all time. He showed courage on the streets, joining thousands of others in helping the afflicted. He grieved for the dead and exhorted the living. Most of all, in a situation that desperately called for leadership, he led. The crisis required minute-by-minute decisions of grave consequence and for which the rich history of New York City provided no precedents. He acted decisively. He was in charge, in command, from the first moments of crisis until he left office. Like a general on the front lines, he spoke to the world from the streets of New York, calmly factual and intensely emotional.

Given that bravura performance, it seems almost pointless to ask New Yorkers whether they approved of his job as mayor. But they were asked and, to no one's surprise, the previously troubled mayor emerged as a public hero.[1] George Pataki, governor of New York, also had a role to

---

[1] A CBS/*New York Times* poll of New Yorkers on October 12, 2001, found 94 percent of Democrats and 98 percent of Republicans expressing approval of Giuliani's crisis performance. National polls produced similar numbers.

play in the aftermath of 9/11. And his approval from the voters of New York State also soared, up by twenty points. Charles Schumer, senior senator from New York, notched a thirteen-point gain around the terrorism events. The more controversial junior senator, Hillary Clinton, gained even more, seventeen.

The governors of other states had a lesser role. It fell to them to issue statements of sympathy and to do what little other legal jurisdictions could do to aid New York in need. Notwithstanding their lesser roles, the governors' net approval also soared. Between August and September 2001, average approval for the fourteen sitting governors whose approval was assessed before and after 9/11 increased by nine points, by far the largest one-month gain ever recorded. Between August and October, Gray Davis in far-off California saw his standing rise by seventeen points. Jane Swift in Massachusetts gained sixteen between July and October. Gains were registered by Taft in Ohio, Easley in North Carolina, McCallum in Wisconsin, Perry in Texas. And so it went.[2] Governors somehow became more sympathetic figures, even when they had little role in the events that so moved the public.

Reaction to the events of 9/11 was to give President George W. Bush the largest increase in public approval ever recorded. Although the magnitude still impresses, the public response was far from unprecedented. That is how Americans respond to the chief executive in times of national crisis – a well-worn piece of political lore. Unlike smaller moments of crisis in our history, this one fundamentally altered the Bush presidency. Following the terrorism events and fed by support for Bush's actions against the terrorist base of operations in Afghanistan, there was a surge of public support that had not fully dissipated a year later.

Senators suddenly became more popular too. Legislative bodies have little independent role in a crisis, their chief duty being to support executive calls to action. That they did, passing bills to aid New York City, the "Patriot" Act to assist the investigation of terrorism, and supporting Bush's Afghanistan war. The Senate, controlled by the opposition Democrats, saw its net approval (the average approval of individual senators) rise by over ten points in the month after 9/11, the opposition Democrats gaining even more than Bush's Republicans.

Many survey organizations regularly ask about Congress and regularly find that Americans don't think much of their most democratic branch.

---

[2] Perhaps ironically, the president's brother Jeb in Florida was among those not much affected, gaining a single point.

Asked whether they "approve or disapprove of the way the Congress is doing its job," the American public often finds much to disapprove. Its view was almost neutral, with 49 percent of those expressing a non-neutral opinion approving in August 2001. After the September terrorism, it went to 63 percent approving and by October was at 78 percent. Congress, after 9/11, was no longer a "public enemy."[3] And it was not only Congress. Trust in government, in general, soared in 2001 to levels never before seen; the number asserting trust more than doubling after September 11.

We don't know about most individual members of Congress. Congressional districts are unmatched to normal survey sampling units. Nor do we know about lesser state officials or the huge numbers of people who administer local government. But clearly there was a pattern in the public response to terrorism. People are asked how a body such as Congress, or the president, senators, or governors are doing their jobs. When the response is so uniform, as it was after 9/11, that response must reflect something more than simple personnel evaluation. That something is a change in how people feel about government in all its aspects. It is a dynamic in which people reevaluate long-standing prejudices and draw on new considerations.

People do not normally think about public life, do not care much whether their senator or governor is doing a good job. That doesn't have much to do with daily life. Crisis changes that. It makes people look to government to act and notice when it has acted. The government they see is both unified and responsive to public demands, and they like those things.

POLICY PREFERENCES

Consider a story devoid of crisis, just normal American politics. The American public was ready in the late 1970s to see government scaled back, to do less of what it did. After the Vietnam War and then the Watergate scandal vacated the center stage of American politics, people began to experience a long-delayed reaction to the government-expanding policies of the 1960s. They began to want less of what government was doing.

Spending on domestic priorities, education, environment, cities, health care, and so forth is popular. Many more people usually advocate doing more than less. And so it was in the late 1970s. In 1977, asked about

---

[3] The phrase is from *Congress as Public Enemy* (Hibbing and Theiss-Morse 1996).

spending on education, for example, 48 percent said it was too little and only 10 percent said too much. On environment it was 48 to 11. But perspective is everything here. These are low points; support for doing more was usually stronger. On other issues the numbers were different, but the pattern was the same. Spending was popular on average, but its popularity was at a low point in the final years of the 1970s and in the 1980 election year.

Ronald Reagan sought a mandate to cut taxes and spending and believed that his 1980 triumph over Jimmy Carter gave him one. In early 1981 he cut taxes. And at the same time he trimmed back the growth rates of domestic programs,[4] pretty much across the board, building in new spending on defense programs at the same time. The voters seemed to have spoken and they seemed to have gotten what they said they wanted. Taxes were cut and domestic spending was restrained, both important changes in direction for America.

By 1982 a new General Social Survey study, asking the same questions of a new sample, found support for more education spending moving to 56 percent (from 53% in 1980, the last previous study). A three-point movement is about at the limit we can expect from chance fluctuation and thus would not be taken as a signal of important movement. On environmental questions preferences also moved toward more spending, but by only two points. The 1983 study found another three-point gain on education and four on environment. These one-year movements are easy to write off. Just a few points, just a few issues. But the pattern was quite general. On most of the things that could tap basic attitudes toward government, you would see the same two- or three- or four-point changes from one year to the next. And when you put the years back to back, the size of the changes can no longer be ascribed to chance. But they don't yet connote a trend.

But a trend was indeed under way. Something was going on out in the country. Millions of people, having moved away from supporting government spending in the late 1970s, were moving back in support in the 1980s. Those millions were barely perceptible in the survey numbers and hardly noticed in Washington. The percentages of those who thought that "too little" was being spent on education moved from 60 in 1983 to 64 in 1984, down to 60 in 1985, then 61 in 1986, 62 in 1987, 64 in 1988.

---

[4] The Reagan domestic budget revisions were called "cuts," by both Reagan and his opponents, but in most cases they were cuts from projected growth rates, not absolute reductions in dollar spending.

And the opposite numbers advocating "too much" fell at the same time. Over the eight years of the Reagan administration the percentages moved from 53 to 10 (83% "too little") to 64 to 4 (94%). On environment it was the same, moving from 48 to 17 (74%) in 1980 to 65 to 5 (93%) at the close of the administration.

Then Vice President Bush, seeking to succeed Reagan in 1988, was one of those who noticed the movement in sentiment. He declared his brand of conservatism "kinder and gentler" – and did not have to say kinder and gentler than who's. The relative conservatism that had been an asset to Reagan in 1980 was not there for Bush, who wisely shifted the agenda to the symbolic side of liberalism – race and civil liberties in particular – because there was no leverage in attacking the operational side of liberalism: expansive government domestic programs.

With a conservative, albeit "kinder and gentler" president in the White House, the trend out in the country continued. On issue after issue, the movement during Bush's four years was the same: away from conservatism and toward liberalism. Opinions were in motion across the sweep of issue concerns called the New Deal, the welfare state, or big government. People wanted more government. "Big government" itself is not a popular symbol. But the things of which it is composed were popular. "I am for a smaller, leaner government," people would say, except for education, except for the environment, except for urban mass transit, except on racial equality, except Social Security (and of course Medicare), except health care, gun control, and on and on. Even the always unloved welfare programs drew substantially more support by the end of Bush's term than they had twelve years before. The exceptions were nearly all the things that government did.[5]

When George Bush sought a second term in 1992 these little changes that went mostly unnoticed had created an electorate dramatically more like that which had elected John Kennedy and Lyndon Johnson than anything seen in the subsequent three decades. It was an uphill struggle against Bill Clinton, who wanted to put government to work addressing problems that people cared about. Bush also had an unhappy economic legacy. Although the national economy was starting to turn during 1992, voters were pessimistic. But it did not help that Bush's proposals to do better were based on a conservatism that no longer worked with the public.

---

[5] But in the whole panoply of domestic concerns there were two genuine exceptions to the liberalizing trend: abortion (on which there was no movement at all) and crime, where attitudes continued to shift toward the punitive end of the scale.

The slow shift of public opinion is one of the central forces of American politics. Very different and very much less noticed than the quick responses to election year momentum or to national crisis, opinion moved by the accretion of ordinary people's experience with politics is so slow one can barely see it, so powerful that nothing stands in its way.

In three stories about opinion change one thing is constant. In all three, opinion moves. Important things happen in politics because opinion at one time is different from what it was earlier. But though motion is constant, its pace is very different. The dynamic of response to crisis can begin in minutes. America was different by dinnertime on September 11 than it had been at breakfast. Responses to the cumulative successes and failures of government are more leisurely, taking weeks and months. And the dynamic of changing preferences is so glacial that its evidence takes multiple years to leave a visible path.

This book is about all three dynamics. It is about how public opinion ebbs and flows over time, what moves it, why it moves, and what we can understand about predicting and explaining those movements. Imagine an eddy on top of a wave riding on a tide and you have a picture of public opinion flows in American politics. Some movement is slow and fundamental, some quick and responsive. The day-to-day usually doesn't matter much. But it does when it is the final act of the election drama. There trends of a day or two, taken at the *right* day or two, can be as consequential in impact as movements of a decade. Movements that take decades to run to completion have cumulative effects of fundamental consequence.

SO, WHAT'S NEW?

Survey researchers have been out in the field asking ordinary people their views for about seven decades or so, doing it regularly and seriously for about five. So what is there that we don't already know? In fact, we haven't known much at all about how public opinion moves, how, if at all, it responds to the events of politics or whether its movements are consequential.

Part of why we haven't known these things is that the early decades of opinion research were characterized by an implicit belief that opinions were more or less fixed. Not knowing anything at the outset about how people responded to politics and what they believed, it was reasonable to assume there was a fixed reality out there in want of description. So opinion researchers set out to do that description, imagining all the different questions that might elicit different pieces of the opinion jigsaw puzzle. It was a necessary first step. It appears that they sought to cover the ground as thoroughly as possible, imagining all the different questions that might be asked. And it also appears (and this is more surmise than fact) that they regarded asking the same question more than once as a wasted opportunity, and perhaps even akin to plagiarism. Researchers were supposed to write their own questions, not use those that had previously been used.[6]

Thus the early decades of opinion research produced no evidence of opinion change, the first requisite of which is repeating the same queries over time. It takes many years of measuring things before we have rich enough data to see movements. Imagine forecasting the weather if what we had for data were one or two or three or four measurements of key variables (and with so few measurements, we wouldn't know what was key). The whole story of weather is dynamic, how pressure systems interact with jet streams and heat and moisture sources to produce the rain or shine we see. Take away those dynamics, and what is left is a forecast that today might look a lot like yesterday, but also it might not!

That's about where we have been in politics. We know the dynamics matter, but we are only beginning to have enough measures to study them. We are beginning to learn about opinion dynamics. Much of what we know we have learned in the last decade.[7] That work is not particularly accessible, because it is burdened with thousands of details, each question treated as a thing in itself. Imagine having thousands of temperature, pressure, and wind-speed movements and having to figure out what they mean. They are ultimately the data required by rich understandings of meteorology, but as raw data they aren't very useful. To arrive at a forecast

---

[6] A technical issue, the form of question wording, also had a pernicious influence on evidence of opinion change. Early studies relied heavily on the "Likert" question format, where an assertion is read and then the respondent is asked to agree or disagree with it. Because people's opinions were so lightly held (see Chapter 2), they tended to agree with the assertions much more often than disagree. We now understand that we were dealing with the absence of real opinions, a situation in which plausible-sounding assertions easily convince the respondent to agree. Since we were creating opinions on the spot, in addition to measuring them, the questions were poor measures of real opinion. When that was recognized, survey organizations began to use variations on a forced choice format, which produces better data. The style is to take two opposite, but plausible sounding assertions, pair them, and then have the respondent choose between them. The question wording, "Some people think . . . whereas others think . . ." encourages respondents to think that both are reasonable positions so as not to tip the response one way or the other. When organizations began to use these other formats, all the early work using Likert questions was orphaned because the two question forms do not produce comparable answers.

[7] See, in particular, Stimson 1991, 1998; Mayer 1992; Page and Shapiro 1992; Zaller 1992; Wlezien 1995; Kellstedt 2000; and Erikson, MacKuen, and Stimson 2002.

we care about, the raw data have to be digested. That has been the state of public opinion: lots of raw data.

Recording meteorological data taxes the technological capacity of data storage; there is so much of it. Public opinion is not that overwhelming. But still, the raw data for this book, displayed as questions and answers in a table for each, would run to perhaps 20,000 pages of detail. And this is the data aggregated for the nation. A display of raw data, what each respondent said to each question, begins to rival the proportions of documenting the weather. The dominant style of writing about public opinion displays those national sample aggregates, called "marginals," short for "marginal totals." It says, on issue after issue, "in response to the question . . . ," " *x* percent said *y*." The flood of detail quickly surpasses reader interest.

On top of that the work on opinion dynamics is technical, a critique that applies squarely to my own contributions as well as those of others. What we have done in the last decade begins to tell the story of opinion dynamics in real politics, but most of the people who care about real politics would not want to read it. It is too full of the apparatus of social research, lengthy tomes on concepts, measures, and analytic designs. These things are all necessary, but they aren't anyone's idea of good reading, and they are for all practical purposes inaccessible to most of those who care about understanding politics.

This book is for readers who care about politics and want to know how politics is driven by opinion dynamics. Everything in it is based on the scientific work on concepts, measures, analyses, and tests, but it is written without the overlay of social science.

As a means to be both comprehensive and readable, most treatment of opinion in this book is summaries of multiple indicators. It combines numerous questions with similar focus on topics. Sometimes these are as narrow as the level of involvement of the federal government in, say, education, sometimes as broad as just basic liberalism or conservatism of domestic policy preferences across the board. That gets us away from those tens of thousands of pages of raw data and also presents full movements in regular time series as opposed to the raw data, which are spotty and irregular. Instead of thousands of pressure readings – to continue our weather metaphor – we'll see isobar maps. The one presents the same data as the other, but the latter is a simple picture of what matters instead of the overwhelming detail.

This is unusual in writing about public opinion, where there is great skepticism about combining and generalizing the results of surveys. That skepticism results from the excesses of our past when, not realizing how sensitive question wording could be, analysts combined information from different series and ended up creating artificial movements, apparent trends that were due to the change of question wording, not real change of opinion. The reader is going to have to trust that I do not do that. And I don't. Having spent years developing a technology to estimate the dimensions of opinion that underlie survey responses – the isobars from the pressure readings – I am sensitive to question comparability issues, which are fully under control in these analyses.[8]

Note the occasional use of the adjective "domestic." That reflects a basic fact of American public opinion, that the domestic policy agenda is fundamentally different from foreign policy. While many things that seem separate are seen to move together, domestic and foreign opinions do not. Foreign policy controversies engage considerations entirely different from the domestic realm. All of the analysis that follows is about domestic politics.

A THEORY OF PUBLIC OPINION

Ordinary people are ignorant *and* calculating about politics. They know so little about public life that it is often hard to tell something from nothing, to find any fact-based beliefs. And they have goals, private and public, they think a little about how to achieve them, and they act on their thoughts. Usually these two sides of human behavior, ignorant and calculating, are forced into confrontation. We want people to be ignorant and irrational, on the one hand, or informed and calculating, on the other. It makes for a consistent view of the human condition. But it is wrong.

Both poles of consistency have failed to square with the evidence. "Informed and calculating" was first to go. We believed, before we seriously got about the business of studying ordinary people, that we would find in them the democratic citizens that our quasi-religious commitment to democracy demanded. We thought they would have views like the participants of a Georgetown cocktail party, that they would take one side or the other of public debates and would have a system of beliefs, perhaps even a public philosophy, that would support their positions.[9]

---

[8] To keep the book about politics, the dimensional technology itself does not appear in these pages. The technologically curious can see Chapter 3 and the appendix of Stimson 1998.

[9] Of course, we can't really know what "we" thought about public opinion in an era in which no systematic study was possible. Surely, elected politicians must always have

Such a view survived a couple thousand years of speculation about the public. Its death was quick and brutal when early students of public opinion actually went out and interviewed ordinary people in surveys. The tone of astonishment of these first reports is testimony to the wild unreality of the portrait we expected to see. What those studies found was that ordinary Americans knew almost nothing about public affairs and appeared to care about issues as much as they knew: almost not at all. Their beliefs were a scattering of unrelated ideas, often mutually contradictory. Structure was nowhere to be found. Almost equally astonishing is the fact that most cared little about the views they politely professed in response to interviewer's questions. They said so. And their behavior backed up the claim. Confronted with any counterargument, they would change sides. The early analysts were terrified to discover that this shallowness of opinion holding was so great that innocent choices to use one word rather than another in survey questions would have large effects on the answers obtained.

The scientific study of public opinion began roughly at the same time as did the Cold War between East and West. One of the early findings was that most Americans, asked about "Russia," were not as hostile as would have been expected from the times. Posing the same question about the "Soviet Union," in contrast, produced the expected antagonism. And if the adjective "Communist" were added to the label, the answers were so one-sided as to make the questions unworkable; they produced only a single response. And yet these were all the same question. Thus, opinions were so lightly held that they were strongly influenced by the shape of the question asked. And this beyond doubt was the most intense issue of the times.

And we learned also that mere willingness to express a view did not indicate intensity of feeling. We found that people would also answer nonsense questions. Asked, for example, to express their feelings of warmth or coldness toward people and groups, many respondents proved willing also to express feelings toward individuals and groups that did not exist. And the numbers who rated the nonexistent were not notably smaller than those expressing a view about real people and real groups.

On close analysis, it also became apparent that inconsistency was the hallmark of public opinion. Not only was it the case that people were inconsistent in expressed views toward objects that informed observers

---

known that philosophy had limited power to win elections. We know this to be true from the simplistic appeals that have characterized political campaigns throughout history.

thought went together. That conundrum could be explained by clever theories about the nature of consistency. But Converse's (1964) classic demonstration that inconsistency was also widespread in people's answers to the same questions over time had no easy escape. Converse concluded that much of expressed public opinion was what he called "nonattitudes," the doorstep creation of survey responses by respondents who had no true opinions at all. Because the creation of nonattitudes was essentially a random process, it yielded a different random result on each occasion, an explanation of over-time inconsistency. (This is a conclusion I revisit.)

Thus it seemed obvious that citizens were completely inept, totally unprepared to play their expected role in a democracy. It is hard to overstate the evidence of public ignorance, hard to express the analyst's initial despair at finding out what isn't known by people on the street. Everyone who has looked at survey data on public knowledge and preference has experienced it. The gap between what democracy seems to demand of voters and what voters supply is just immense.

It was natural in the face of this evidence to conclude, as most early analysts did, that voters were beyond understanding as rational actors. If they knew almost nothing of public affairs, it was an easy step to conclude further that they were pawns in the game of politics, bereft of real preferences and unable to calculate the consequences of their acts.

The conclusion that seemed to follow – that citizens act without purpose or calculation in politics – will also turn out to be wrong. But showing that first requires developing some structure.

SOME POSTULATES ABOUT OPINION MOVEMENT

I pause here to lay out some fundamentals, what I believe to be generally true about public opinion. The purpose is to construct the view of movements that will underlie the rest of the book. These are the building blocks.

Some People Some of the Time Pay Attention to Government

"Some" is not a powerful word. In formal logic it means "at least one." I can satisfy that all by myself. But I mean more. I mean "some" as in "enough to matter." I mean nontrivial numbers. Perhaps it is on the order of saying that over a given period of time at least 10 percent care about *something* that the government does and at some unusual times large numbers care about something unusually important or visible.

Politics does not require full-time spectators. Nobody needs to pay attention to everything that stimulates debate in the Washington community. And I don't assume that every citizen will care about even one thing. A society doesn't need and maybe couldn't even tolerate that level of involvement. How much attention is necessary for a meaningful interaction? All that is required is that the very most visible acts of, say, a year or a presidential term draw the attention of some small number of people.

We can quantify some of this. We know that nontrivial numbers of Americans subscribe to news-laden national newspapers such as the *New York Times* or the *Wall Street Journal* and that larger numbers watch serious news programs on television such as *NewsHour* on PBS or are informed by the excellent news coverage of National Public Radio.[10] And some actually read the news portions of their daily local papers and not merely the funnies, horoscopes, advice to the lovelorn, and sports. And we know something about the peak involvement of normally inattentive people. About half of all Americans vote once every four years, something over 30 percent at least once every two years. Presidential debates are infrequent, but have large viewership when they occur. At the outer extreme, the crisis of September 11 and its aftermath engaged virtually all living Americans.

The point of this excursion is this: The overwhelming evidence of lack of interest and involvement in public affairs by ordinary Americans is indisputable. But the conclusion that *nobody* pays attention does not follow. Some people some of the time pay attention to government.

Some People Some of the Time Care What Government Docs

Paying attention does not imply caring (although paying attention does impose an opportunity cost, time that might have been spent doing something else, which does imply motivation of some sort). Many people say that they don't care who wins elections. But there is evidence that some do. The long recount of the Bush versus Gore contest in Florida carried news ratings for almost two months in 2000. (But we shouldn't get carried away here; it was no match for the O. J. Simpson trial.) But the assumption is safe: Some people some of the time care what government does.

A much larger number of people, essentially everybody, cares about the things government *doesn't* do. What government doesn't do is of course

---

[10] Larger numbers, of course, watch network and cable news programs, where political news is intermixed with much ratings-driven shock and entertainment material.

an infinite list of possibilities, which have the common feature that they are deeply unpopular.

The public would be excited, often opposed, to radical changes in American life and politics. Politicians know this, of course, and consequently do not propose truly radical changes. So long as they restrict public debate to little changes around the edges, most citizens are comfortable ignoring the daily flow of public activity.

People care about abortion, for example, pro and con. We have a continuing discussion about changes in the abortion law. Proposals are things on the order of requiring parental consent for under-age women seeking an abortion. This excites the subset of people interested in public issues or just this one, but its importance is mainly symbolic: If it passes or fails, it is a victory for one side of the debate and hints that future policy changes might go in the same direction. Most Americans are tuned out of this debate. Even though they care about abortion, they don't care enough to get involved in the back-and-forth over changes at the margin.

Now imagine that politicians get serious about the issue and go all the way, completely eliminating legal abortion or (less drastically) completely eliminating all legal impediments to abortion rights. Would most Americans care about this change? They would. We could reasonably expect huge public response and truly sweeping political repercussions. Thus the potential to care about radical changes, however hypothetical (because we don't witness radical changes), is a quite real curb on politicians' behavior.[11]

Some of Those Who Pay No Attention to Government Will Nonetheless Form Public Opinions

Without any information flow whatsoever on the topic of politics (or just about anything else), one can form a view of what is good or bad simply by adopting the views of someone else who does pay attention. This process is everywhere. We all engage in specialization of labor, paying attention to a small number of things that we find interesting and pretty much ignoring

---

[11] The evidence for the point is on the order of the dog that famously didn't bark. In the era in which the parties have aligned themselves for and against abortion, they have produced white-hot campaign rhetoric on the issue. But given unified control of government, both have backed away from the positions of campaign rhetoric and instead engaged in the normal politics of marginal change, Democrats proposing restrictions on demonstrators at abortion clinics, Republicans proposing to allow states freedom to curtail abortion rights in certain fairly restrictive circumstances.

everything else. If we are then called on to form a view of the "everything else" and we know someone who does pay some attention, someone we like and trust, we simply adopt his or her views. It is a sensible thing to do. For if the thing to be evaluated is in the category "not important enough to pay attention to," then adopting the views of a trusted person is smarter than the alternatives of flipping a coin or paying the cost of being informed.

Thus those who pay no attention to government or politics will sometimes have political opinions. Such opinions will often not appear orderly with regard to other things the person knows or believes, for they didn't in fact come from the person in question. But if you adopt someone else's view of politics – and the view adopted was responsive to what was going on in Washington – then notwithstanding the broken line of cause and effect, *your view will be orderly, responsive to what really happened.* Thus we may conclude that the set of those who hold orderly public views will include both those who pay attention and some of those who do not.

Much Public Opinion Is Media-Influenced

We regularly argue along partisan and ideological lines about media slant toward one or the other side in American politics. But arguments about slant miss the important action. When the media carry debates between forceful opponents, we don't expect to find media influence, and the evidence pretty much says that there is little.[12] But it is quite wrong to assume that all issues get two-sided treatment. There are many matters where one side is dominant and is the only message the public hears.

"Government," for example, is always a villain, never a hero of media stories. That is because the press assigns itself the role of watchdog, taking seriously the responsibility of reporting misdeeds in the public order. The press has no responsibility to be balanced on this matter. And stories that reported wise, virtuous, and efficient government activities would usually fail the criteria of newsworthiness. On government waste, politicians get into the act too. Conservatives rail about welfare, liberals about defense, and what the public hears from both sides is that government is wasteful. There is no debate about whether there is waste; the debate is only about

---

[12] What the evidence does show, however, is that media play an influential role in setting the public agenda by choosing to cover some issues and not others. The common statement is that media do not tell people what to think, but they do tell them what to think about. See Kellstedt (2003) for an extension of this idea into the matter of shaping opinions about race.

where waste is to be found. And then in politics, "waste" comes to mean "money spent on purposes I don't like," as opposed to the normal financial connotation, that is, money spent that does not serve any purpose.

The president of the United States has friends and foes. The friends will vigorously defend his or her performance in office.[13] Congress, in contrast, has only foes. There is no public voice raised in the defense of the institution. Indeed, Richard Fenno (1978) reports that members of Congress are among its most vociferous and consistent critics. "That place is a mess," they say to their constituents. "Send me there to straighten it out." That Congress is usually unloved doesn't require much explanation.

Many of the goals of government programs are so popular that one side of a potential debate censors itself. Americans revere good education and a clean environment, for example. But even though education and environment programs have opponents, those opponents steer clear of public opposition. Those, for example, who want to limit activities in education will argue around the edges, that the programs are flawed, that money is wasted, and so forth. What they do not argue (because they know the argument is a loser) is that education isn't worth the money. Environmental regulation is attacked as bureaucratic, wasteful, insensitive to economic realities, and so forth. But no one will argue in public that a clean environment isn't worth the cost.

The real slant in all these cases comes from self-censorship. The problem isn't merely that coverage of the debate reflects only one side; it is that only one side is publicly aired. The press cannot (and should not) create debates that do not exist. We tend to think of politics always as two-sided and assume that political issues will usually produce two-sided debates. But it is not in the self-interest of real politicians to defend unpopular positions. So two-sided issue debates are not universal; they tend to occur only in cases where the issue is framed such that the two sides are about equally numerous and popular.

The result of one-sided debates is what all would expect. Public opinion reflects only that one side. And this is circular: Because one side is more popular, only that side is heard, and that makes it even more popular, which makes it less likely that the other side will be heard, and on and on. It would be useful for the public order if this were not true. It would be helpful to have even-handed assessments of how much education or environment are worth, whether government is actually wasteful, whether

---

[13] Richard Nixon, in his final days in office, illustrates the limit of the assertion. That one president at that one time had no public friends.

Congress is congenitally stupid, and so forth. But in a market system where the coinage is votes, that is not going to happen.

In each of the cases I have illustrated there is an ideological slant that results, left or right. What can we say in sum? Because what the public wants to hear determines which positions are self-censored, we can reasonably expect the net effect of one-sided treatments to be neutral relative to public opinion. The bias is toward the middle. Arguments that divide more or less at the center of public opinion get aired in the public media. Ideas and positions that, whatever their intellectual merit, cannot draw majority support are systematically suppressed by self-interested politicians, who wage their wars on fronts where they can win.

These postulates about information and opinion are static; they inform us about who might have actual opinions, how numerous they are, and what those opinions might be. Now think about the public, the aggregate of all those individual views. Think of it as an *it*. And now I ask, how does it move over time? What can we learn about how the public responds to political events from what we know?

Opinion Dynamics: Change in Response to Events

When we ask what happens to this aggregate public and what properties it has, the result will be counterintuitive for many readers. The result will be opinion movements that are almost totally dominated by the orderly responses of those who pay some attention. The electorate, the aggregate of the people, will display a wholly orderly response to government. How can this be? What is the sleight-of-hand that pulls this rabbit from the magician's hat? The answer is two-fold: It is the mathematics of aggregation gain and it is opinion leadership by the better informed.

Aggregation Gain
Aggregation accentuates the orderly over the disorderly, the signal over the noise. When you sum up the patterns in which people respond to events, some will be common – many people responding the same way at the same time – and many will be idiosyncratic. Multiple "copies" of responses that are similar gain force; they add up. Idiosyncratic (or random) responses do not add up; they tend to cancel one another. If some rats in a maze run toward the food and others go off in random directions, the average for all is toward the food. If some people become more conservative when government undertakes liberal actions and others respond randomly, then the public on average becomes more conservative.

Notice that the argument is about orderly, not correct behavior. Aggregation will accentuate anything that is regular; it has no will, no consciousness to select better over worse. AM radio is built on the principle of aggregation gain; that is what allows plucking a weak signal out of an environment filled by static. But if the wrong signal is at the frequency you tune to – a nearby station or maybe your neighbor's garage door opener – that wrong signal, also orderly, also gets amplified.

The conclusion I have been building to is this: if just some people pay attention to politics and just some care a little bit about it – never mind all those who don't pay attention and don't care – the average of opinions will predominantly reflect those who pay attention and care. It is precisely this average we see when we see *public* opinion.

Opinion Leadership

Imagine a perverse specialization of labor in which the uncaring and uninformed were as likely to influence the views of the caring and informed as vice versa. That would weaken the orderliness of opinion, sometimes replacing the orderly with the random. But of course specialization of knowledge has a logic that leads to the reverse. Those who have knowledge are more likely to influence those who don't than the other way around. We say, "I haven't paid any attention to x and now I need to make a decision about it. I wonder who can tell me what to do?" We seek to be influenced when we don't know or care very much. We are so accustomed to politics as seeking to influence, as people pressing their views on others, that it is easy to forget the reality that most people do not care much about politics and do not have views. To avoid the cost of paying attention to a subject that does not interest them, they are happy to be influenced by others. Because people who don't know are likely to be influenced by those who do, their responses are likely to carry the same orderliness as the informed response.

Imagine a little conversation. You say to me, "George W. Bush is too conservative." I don't know what "conservative" means and I don't care about what I don't know. But if I then repeat the claim in a survey or act on it in the voting booth, then your orderly views become mine. Bush's actions produced your orderly response because you understood them. They produced an equally orderly response in me without understanding. When this conversation is repeated a thousand times over, it produces a more orderly public response. "The public" thus becomes much more orderly than the average of individuals. The electorate is a lot smarter than the voters.

The public opinion of this book is orderly. It has patterns, that is, which can be understood as predictable responses to the real world events that it witnesses.[14] That does not mean that it is wise, that its beliefs about facts are correct, or that its judgment is good. There is ample evidence that all these are sometimes false. They are things we would like to believe about public opinion, things that would be supportive of a commitment to democratic ideals. But like the idea that jury verdicts are always correct, it takes an argument from faith, not fact, to make them true.

But just orderly is quite a lot, dramatically contrary to much that is written about public opinion. Because almost everything we know about opinion comes from the study of individual opinion holding, we have hugely underestimated the aggregate order. We have theories that assert that opinion is uninformed (and it is *on average*) and emphasize opinion holding as filling a psychological need. That it might be a simple response to what is going on in politics is a fairly radical assertion, one that can be made only about the orderly aggregate.

Because all that it takes is for some few to pay attention, public opinion becomes more than just orderly; it becomes a sensitive barometer. It moves not only in response to big and exciting events; it also tracks more subtle and normal politics. Because its movements are meaningful, it has a lot to tell us about politics in Washington. Because they are also consequential for elections and policy making – and the evidence is now clear that they are (Erikson et al. 2002) – these movements send a message back in the other direction too.

Public opinion is the drive wheel of American politics in my view and in this book. That is not because many in the public care or that any care very much. All it takes is that some care and then the rest follow. When some care, then events inside the Beltway will produce responses outside it. Those responses are what matters.

DESIGN OF THE BOOK

The focus of Chapter 2 is long-term flows of opinion. I ask what Americans want from government and how that preference moves over decades of political time. The chapter gets beneath the raw data on preferences

---

[14] Page and Shapiro 1992 assert also that it is "rational," that its actions are in part calculated to achieve goals. I am inclined to agree. But I stop short of making that claim myself because (1) the matter of rationality is contentious and pursuing it would require a lengthy discussion, and (2) the evidence for it would have to come from materials beyond the scope of this book. See Erikson et al. 2002.

to observe domains of unified views; how, for example, Americans feel about education or crime or whether to impose controls on handguns. It suggests that these flows move together and that something more basic ties guns to education to welfare and so on.

Chapter 3 takes up the matter of ideology, the bundling of attitudes about many different issues into coherent systems that encapsulate all. It deals particularly with novel issues, asking why they arise and then what happens to them over time. Its theory of issue evolution predicts that the party system eventually converts them into variations of left and right, liberalism and conservatism. The chapter closes with a look at a strange phenomenon of American politics, that conservative symbols are more popular than liberal ones at the same time as liberal views on specific controversies outweigh conservative ones.

Chapter 4 turns to an altogether different sort of dynamics, the day-to-day horse race of the presidential campaign. It focuses on what the polls do and don't mean and on typical patterns of the stretch run and assesses what matters in a presidential campaign, what key events produce winners and losers.

Chapter 5 turns to public response to government between the campaigns, asking what it is that people like and dislike and why there are systematic patterns in approving and disapproving individual officeholders as well as institutions such as Congress. It concludes that approval and trust are a syndrome of attitudes that really have quite little to do with the specific acts of those being evaluated.

Chapter 6 attempts to make sense of the whole. It argues that the emergent intelligence of electorates needs to be understood as a function of how small are the changes necessary to move politics. It reinterprets politics in light of the view that it is a specialized subset of citizens, and not an obvious one, that produces almost all the systematic change in our politics.

2

What the Public Wants from Government

The 1950s were the decade of conformity. We practiced moderation to excess. The sound of the throbbing rhythms of Buddy Holly and his Crickets was just beginning to compete with crooners and Doris Day musicals for American musical tastes. Americans warmed to the grandfatherly Eisenhower and aspired to have kids who were "well rounded."

In politics we feared the new A-bomb. With the Great Depression cured by Roosevelt and by World War II, there was little passion for changing the domestic order, little passion for anything. It was a time of bland.

Public opinion polling, in its childhood but now beyond infancy, was more gimmick and entertainment than science. Surveys covered everything, exploring how Americans felt about everything, politics not being a particularly important part. The Gallup poll regularly explored topics such as, "Who is your favorite girl singer?"

The Michigan election surveys in 1956, seeking responses to the statement, "If Negroes are not getting fair treatment in jobs and housing, the government should see to it that they do," found 61 percent in favor and 19 percent opposed. Two years later the balance was 63 to 18. No one noticed the change. In 1958 the Opinion Research Corporation, asking whether people approved a law that guaranteed the right to form labor unions, found the public divided 74 to 11. Then two years later it was 75 to 9. At about the same time, the Michigan studies found support for government doing something to provide low-cost health care moving from about two-thirds to three-fourths in these same years of the Eisenhower administration. Support for greater government involvement in guaranteeing employment moved from 68 to 69 and then to 71 percent in 1956, 1958, and 1960. Gallup surveys show an uneven trend in acceptance of income tax levels from about 40 percent in 1956 to about 45 percent in 1959. The Gallup organization charted similar movements in support of statehood for Alaska and Hawaii, seen at the time as racial issues.

Nobody saw the change. But here the 1960s were emerging; it was John Kennedy's New Frontier, but long before Kennedy's 1960 election. Americans were changing how they felt about government. They were seeing problems in America and increasingly looking to government to solve them. That change would lay the groundwork for the New Frontier and then Lyndon Johnson's more ambitious Great Society. This was a button-down era, but its progeny would fuel the youth revolution and the counterculture to come.

Nobody remarked on these smallish trends because we didn't know enough then of what to expect of public opinion to take them seriously. We were just beginning to grasp the contours of opinion. We weren't sure whether we would find support for, say, labor unions, in the 60 or 80 percent range. In that context small movements in one direction just didn't draw attention.

What is a 1 percent movement in a survey? How much can it signify? Well, if we think of a survey as a sample, then 1 percent of a sample of 1,500 (typical for that time) is fifteen people! Fifteen people who once opposed some government action now support it. What can that signify? But the sample is a sample of American citizens, and 1 percent of them (say, of the roughly half who vote) is about a million people. If we were to hear that a million people who once opposed something have switched to supporters, we would think that is a pretty big deal. And that is exactly what those samples tell us, that millions of people were in movement. And that is why those 1 percent movements, well within what reporters like to call a "margin of error," stand for something noteworthy.[1] Taking all those issue trends together we can say that between 1956 and 1960 something like two million American voters moved from opposition to support of the elements of the welfare state. Had we asked about dozens of policy issues, as we now do, instead of just a few, we would have seen a similar movement across these dozens. We would have known that something important was under way.

---

[1] I am ignoring here the issue of statistical inference, whether or not we could be confident that those 1 percent movements were real and not mere random blips. I ignore it both to be nontechnical and because it is not particularly useful to know whether year-to-year movements can be reliably estimated when what matters is the multiyear trends, which are always highly reliable.

The sample, the thing that we can know, is subject to zigs and zags over time from sampling fluctuation. These are errors in our estimation of the thing we care about, but don't know: the population from which the sample was drawn. This population is probably marching calmly in one direction. And before the march is finished, before some new force arises that gets people to change their minds in the opposite direction, that march moves many millions of people from one place to another. In a politics that depends crucially on which side of the line of 50-50 you are on, moving millions of people is usually sufficient. Like football at the goal line, a play that produces mere inches can be the game winner.

The era was maybe not as conservative as its reputation. Eisenhower, after all, stands as the modern Republican who least questioned the welfare state originating in the New Deal. Republican domestic stands of the time were called "me-tooism," saying about each of the popular domestic innovations of FDR and the Democrats, "we support that too." In this context of moderate conservatism the public was in motion toward liberalism. When John Kennedy appealed in his 1960 campaign to "get the country moving again," it was not only the economy that people wanted in motion. There was the beginning of a longing for activist government. The appeal struck a responsive chord.

Such movements are a basic aspect of American politics, relatively little known or studied. It is a subject on which I spend a good deal of time in this book. I want to get beneath the mere data of response to this or that question and capture the feeling of millions of people quietly revising their thinking. The questions and the percentages who say this or that are like ripples in a stream. It is the current that really moves things. The goal of all the analyses to come is finding that current, seeing which way it is running and why. As a starting point I need to explore what this public opinion we measure is, what it says about the people who answer the questions.

THINKING ABOUT PUBLIC OPINION

Although we have done so, it probably isn't wise to just formulate questions about what sort of policies people prefer, ask them, and then interpret the result as the literal truth. Now with the benefit of over half a century of experience, we know that what people say in response to surveys needs to be understood in the context of the mental models used to process questions. We can go quite far wrong if we don't get this right.

Thus I visit this issue, asking what are people thinking about when asked a question about their preferences.

Rehearsed Attitudes

If asked what "we" thought about the nature of public opinion in the earliest decades of opinion research, the true answer would be that we didn't think much about it at all.[2] And that got us into trouble. At the outset the natural assumption about how ordinary people thought about public issues would have been that it was similar to how those who designed surveys thought about public issues. Members of an educated and politically conscious class, the survey designers – mostly a mix of professors and working journalists – were the sort of people who attended to controversies reported in the media, thought about the debates and conflicts, and came down on one side or the other.

The survey designers had what might be called "rehearsed attitudes." That is, they had positions on the issues of the day and were ready to defend them in a cocktail party sort of debate. So did politicians. And so did "the public," as seen, for example, in letters to the editor. And so researchers set out to measure the public's rehearsed attitudes, posing questions such as, "Proposal A would do this and proposal B would do that; which do you prefer?" Since A and B were the sort of positions taken by leading actors in American politics, respondents were expected to have views pro and con.

It turns out that if you pose questions of that sort, most survey respondents will answer them. And if you probe a little, pushing those who say initially that they haven't thought about it or have no view on the matter, even more will produce a response that takes one side or the other. All appears well in this setup until you begin to examine the consistency of various answers.

The survey designers had consistent attitudes; they were liberals or conservatives and knew which packages of ideas went with other packages. The ordinary people who responded to surveys, however, were quite opposite. Most of them displayed such scant evidence of consistency – by any number of alternative criteria – that researchers were both puzzled and dismayed.[3] The puzzling aspect was that such evidence did not at

---

[2] My own earliest foray into opinion research was in the early 1960s, two to three decades after the outset. Hence the quotation marks around "we."

[3] The classic work on issues of belief consistency is in Campbell et al. 1960; the argument is improved and extended in Converse 1964.

all comport with the rational activist view of citizens that was the standard perception of the pre-survey era. (Think of the independent-minded voter so often seen in newspaper editorial pages.) The dismaying aspect was that such citizens seemed almost wholly incapable of playing the role envisioned for them in democratic theory. Voters who seemed to find self-contradiction as appealing as consistency could not communicate their confusing mix of views through their votes.

Converse (1964) finally pushed the consistency evidence to a final, virtually undeniable, conclusion. However people structure their thoughts about politics, he argued, if they had some structure, it would be seen, at minimum, in some consistency of position on the same issues over time. Working with data from 1956, 1958, and 1960, where a national sample of respondents had been asked exactly the same questions about their preferences at multiple times, he observed that the evidence of consistency was just slightly better than would be observed by chance. Correlations between positions taken at one time and positions expressed two or four years later were just barely larger than what would be expected from chance.[4]

Nonattitudes

What could be going on? One possibility was that the voters sampled were simply not smart enough to connect the dots. That explanation had some appeal to the analysts. What Converse proposed as an alternative, the "nonattitudes" thesis, was more flattering to the voters but more threatening to the survey enterprise. The explanation, Converse said, was that much – maybe even most – of what was expressed in response to survey questions was not real. The true situation was that many respondents had no attitudes at all. When pressed in the course of the interview to answer queries, politeness and perhaps some embarrassment at not being politically sophisticated led them to just make up answers from thin air. The course of the interview was a learning situation in which respondents

---

[4] Imagine that people were deciding by the rule, "Flip a coin and if it comes up heads, give the conservative response – if tails, give the liberal one." If they had done so, their inconsistency would be only slightly greater than what Converse observed. The same sort of evidence, test-retest correlations of party identification, where typical respondents *did* have stable positions, showed that the procedure would produce evidence of consistency where it truly existed. I can't do justice to the masterful argument in this brief treatment. Suffice it to say that Converse anticipated all the counterarguments to his dismal conclusion and deftly defeated each of them.

were gradually taught that the interviewer wanted responses and was often dissatisfied when the truth was that the respondent had no attitude. The best way to satisfy the interviewer and the quickest way to end the interview was simply to supply an answer to all questions, whether or not any meaningful attitude was present.[5]

Now we have an explanation for inconsistency, both across issues and over time. If responses are just random creations, devoid of reasoning or emotion, then they will not be consistent with anything, including themselves on previous or future occasions. Part of the lesson learned was that respondents were telling the unvarnished truth when they said they had no views and had not thought about the questions posed. Pushing them to answer anyhow was in effect rejecting the truth and demanding that they instead make up a lie about attitudes they did not hold. The set of people who were likely to report rehearsed attitudes was a small one. And the set of issues on which real attitudes were likely to be expressed was small too.[6]

If one were to abstract a model of the survey response from Converse, it would be that respondents, confronted with a question that calls for rehearsed attitudes, report them if they have them, and make them up if they don't.

Sampling from Competing Considerations

People who are professionally involved in politics take up issue after issue and come down on one side. Not only do they take the "liberal" or "conservative" views of particular issues, they take similar positions on many issues and they *become* liberals and conservatives. They decide on the correct resolution of public issues and adopt it as part of their political identity. Having faced the same generic value trade-off questions in a

---

[5] I have always found this surmise reasonable. Having myself three or four times been a respondent to consumer surveys that I did not find interesting, I have reached a view closer to certainty.

[6] The partial solution to the problem, improving the ratio of wheat to chaff in survey research, is two-fold. On the one hand, we need to focus on general, not specific, issues. Many people will have thought about whether they want government to be larger or smaller, to do more or less in various areas, and so forth. It is when we get into particulars – proposal A versus proposal B – that we are likely to encounter more attitude creation than reporting. Second, issues that are old and familiar are much more likely to engage real attitudes than that which is novel. The latest controversy to come along is often the most newsworthy. Unfortunately, it is also the least likely to provoke a report of meaningful attitudes. The reader can use to same rules to decide what to believe or not believe in reported surveys.

whole host of specific issues, they have a resolved position, one that will surely influence how they deal with future value conflicts of the same sort. This will not be news to the reader, who has probably done the same.

It was natural to think that ordinary citizens were the same. If questions had a liberal and a conservative response, we expected liberals to give the former and conservatives to give the latter. It is how we think about things. But John Zaller (1992) and Zaller and Feldman (1992) bring an important insight to the issue. If political life is not particularly important to most citizens, Zaller and Feldman argue – and demonstrably it is not – then the pressure to resolve value conflicts into one consistent position does not exist. Conflicts do not naturally resolve themselves. They get resolved when we feel pressed to take and defend a position. But the citizen tuned out of politics faces no such pressure. The likely outcome of this situation is for such a citizen to entertain simultaneously "considerations" that are in conflict, to hold dear values that might push one either way on a particular controversy and not to resolve for all time which is dominant and which must give way.

How would such a citizen respond to a survey question? ask Zaller and Feldman. In line with Converse, they see little possibility that many citizens will often have a rehearsed attitude that they can report. Instead, the typical respondent will usually be thinking about a particular public controversy for the first time when asked to state his or her preference. Unlike Converse, they propose a mental process for answering that goes beyond "doorstep opinion," or making it up from whole cloth on the spot. They propose an abbreviated mental search in which the respondent searches his or her memory for a set of values ("considerations") that would be relevant to the answer, in essence, saying, "If I had thought about this issue, which beliefs and orientations that I hold would dictate my response?"

Now two factors that come into play make the result of the search partly, but only partly, predictable. One is that the answer to a question posed in a survey is not very important to the respondent (whose chief motivation will often be to end the interview and get back to what he or she was doing before the disruption). Because the answer is unimportant, the respondent will not do an exhaustive search for considerations but will instead sample one or a few that come to mind easily and quickly.

It is crucial to understand that most citizens hold unresolved "competing considerations." Not liberals or conservatives, they hold some considerations that push in the liberal direction and some that push in the conservative direction. Holding competing considerations combined with a casual sampling process means that most people most of time are capable of giving *either* the liberal or the conservative response to a particular question. In so doing they can be quite sincere, even intense, and still be inconsistent. The inconsistency arises from the near random character of *which* considerations are sampled. Psychological theory suggests that what will "come to mind" most easily are idea elements that are fresh, "on the top of the head." We know that such "freshness" is influenced by factors that have a quasi-random character, most importantly how recently the person has thought about the consideration. Recent thoughts are easier to bring to mind than old ones.[7]

A Zaller-Feldman respondent engaging in a partial search among competing considerations will look much like Converse's nonattitudes respondent. The difference is that responses will be meaningful to the respondent, based on the application of his or her own values to the decision problem. But the near randomness of the search will produce a pattern that appears inconsistent to the outside observer. I think the Zaller-Feldman formulation is a very good one. It dominates my view not just of the question of how respondents in a survey process the challenge of a preference question, but more importantly of the essential character of public opinion, whether private or expressed. The model is realistic, as is the idea that most citizens have not chosen, that they are available to either side of a debate depending fundamentally on priming one or another set of values and framing the way the story is told. This will look like familiar territory to politicians who make their living by learning how to prime the values that work for their side of the debate and not the other. Politics would be much more settled if considerations did not compete in the minds of voters. It is much more interesting when they do.

ABSOLUTE AND RELATIVE

Before we can get to the matter of how opinion moves over time, it is useful to think about what it is that we measure. Overwhelmingly, we measure policy preferences, public beliefs about what the government ought to do

---

[7] One of the reasons this theory is so powerful is that it predicts the idea of "priming," that ideas people have recently been exposed to are likely to dominate evaluations. The evidence for priming effects is quite overwhelming. The subtle introduction of an idea, for example, from an earlier question in a survey, reliably affects reported attitudes. More important, ideas that are "primed" in public discussions in the media will affect real public opinion, not merely opinion measured in survey research. See Kellstedt 2000 and 2003 for an important application of the idea to the politics of race in America.

or not do to ameliorate a problem or to improve the quality of citizens' lives. But government is a moving target. What it does at some times is different from what it does at others. Thus public opinion is usually responsive to what government is doing *at the moment*. That gives it a relative character; it tells us not what citizens want, but rather what they want relative to what government is doing recently.

Such opinions behave like a thermostat in Christopher Wlezien's (1995) account of public opinion. Wlezien's story is cybernetic; it provides for a rational response through feedback rather than direct forward control. I digress a bit here to consider the logic of forward control versus feedback.

Start with the commuter's problem of driving to work on city streets. Although this task is successfully completed every day, imagine the problem of writing a set of instructions so that the commuter's car could be programmed to make the drive itself. Just getting the directions right – turn left here, bear 30 degrees to the right when the street splits, and so on – is a considerable task. But programming the car to stay in the proper lane and to negotiate turns is truly difficult. The commuter him- or herself, in contrast, does this twice a day, scarcely processing a remembered thought because it is so nearly automatic.

If we ask why the problem is easy for the driver and nearly impossible to program in advance, the main part of an answer is that most of the driver's control comes from response to feedback. The driver can't give instructions for how to negotiate a particular turn because he or she doesn't actually know, for example, how many degrees of movement on the steering wheel are required. Our driver doesn't *need* to know. As every student driver learns the first time out, you just turn the wheel a little and then observe whether the car is tracking appropriately or veering to one side or the other. When you see evidence of being off course – negative feedback – you respond in real time to the observed error, a correction process so easy and natural that we don't even need to be aware that we are doing it. The consequence is that our commuter gets to work every day without being able to give a precise description of how the feat was accomplished.

The digression is instructive for thinking about how a citizen might control public policy. How much should we spend on environmental regulation this year? Should we acquire a new weapons system for the military or would it be better to put the same money into development of a more advanced system for future acquisition? What rules should we impose on how health care providers will be reimbursed for the services they render under the Medicare program? These are questions of the same order of difficulty as writing a set of instructions for the car to execute. Answers require truly awe-inspiring knowledge, knowledge that could come only from full-time attention to each issue alone. For the citizen who is supposed to go about daily life doing some useful job while others run the government, it is quite impossible to imagine overcoming this information problem. And there goes the hope of democratic governance, down the drain. The citizen who can't know his or her own preferences cannot enforce government action on them.

But allow people to use negative feedback and the problem is immensely simplified. Take the issue of how much to spend on environmental enforcement. I not only do not know the answer, but also can't even quite imagine what I would do to get one. But I get two kinds of feedback every year; how the environment seems to be doing, well or badly, and how painful is it to pay taxes, tolerable or intolerable. From these and nothing more I can easily make a relative judgment. Even though I do not know how much we are currently spending, I can use my preferences (clean environment and low taxes) to give an intelligent answer to the question: Should we do more, less, or about the same as the current effort?

Public opinion in Wlezien's account is of the character of a household thermostat. How warm should the house be? We don't quite know. But if we sense that it is too cold, we send a signal: Turn on the furnace. After the furnace has run for a while and house is getting warmer, we send another signal: That's enough, turn it off. And this very simple device succeeds in enforcing our preferences for how warm we want to be.

If opinion is in some sense thermostatic, that implies that questions about public preferences should be of the same character: "Should we do more, less, or about the same as the current effort?" (Turn on the furnace, the A/C, or do nothing?) There are two sorts of evidence that might suggest whether or not the thermostatic conception is on point. One is what questions survey designers choose to ask. Do the designers think in the relative terms of the thermostat or ask for absolute preferences? They do some of both, so that doesn't settle the issue. The second criterion is of validity: How informative are the answers we get? Here the evidence, some of which is in this chapter, is clear. The relativistic kinds of queries about preferences do a better job of allowing people to express their preferences for government action.

Take gun control as an illustration. Survey organizations fielded absolute questions during the debate over the "Brady" bill in the 1990s. They were of the character, "Should there be a national law that requires a waiting period for the purchase of a handgun? (Yes or no, agree or disagree). The relativistic alternative would be on the order of, "For controlling the purchase of handguns, should the rules be stricter than they currently are, less strict, or about the same as they are now?" Questions of the latter sort consistently carry more information about preferences. They are more highly associated with other attitudes and more predictive of behavior. And, not trivially, they make democracy possible. The homeowner with a thermostat need not understand the physics of home heating and cooling.[8] All that is required is to notice "too hot" or "too cold" and to send the appropriate signal.

MEANS AND ENDS

Most of the "ends" of politics are noncontroversial. It is the means, what government ought to do, that usually produce disagreement. Because ends are usually not controversial, support for them is usually not measured. Posing questions in a survey is an expensive matter. So survey designers wisely choose not to ask people whether they prefer peace to war or prosperity to hard times.

But occasionally, ends themselves generate controversy (and therefore measures of the controversy). Cases that come to mind are issues that pit traditional values supportive of inequality of various kinds, rooted in the old order, against a new assertion of equality. This happens when we are in the midst of real value change. Three such controversies have been prominent in American politics in the last half-century. One was whether or not we should integrate a then quite racially segregated society.

Racial issues, beginning roughly with the civil rights movement of the early 1960s, generated a tangle of conflicts, most still unresolved. But one was the fundamental question of whether a segregated or integrated society was the preferred outcome. Along with a host of conflicts about what government ought to do, there was genuine disagreement about the end goal of integration. (And unlike the current situation where political correctness stifles honest discussion of racial policies, before the success of the civil rights movement very large numbers of Americans were willing to express a preference for a segregated society.)

---

[8] Our homeowner does need to understand something of dynamics, though. Negative feedback works correctly only with patient, incremental responses to feedback. The driver who overcorrects when off-course ends up in the ditch. The impatient homeowner who adjusts the thermostat up when chilly and then down again every time it gets too warm never finds comfort.

While Americans argued about racial integration and racial equality in the early 1960s, the unequal status of women was pretty much taken for granted by both sides. From Biblical times women had been homemakers and child-rearers, venturing occasionally into the workplace, where inferior opportunities were an accepted fact – an accepted fact, it is important to add, by both genders. That was the way things were. Under the law, in the workplace, and in the family, women's role was not merely different, it was inferior. "All men," after all, were "created equal." All of this was challenged, beginning roughly in the middle 1960s, by the women's movement. Comfortable with the gender status quo before the new demand for equality, both women and men became uncomfortable and began to change long-held views.[9]

The third, most recent, and least resolved, such controversy is the demand by newly out-of-the-closet gays and lesbians that they be treated with respect and equality. The traditional view, rooted in religious teachings, held homosexuality to be sin and perversion, rightly the subject of discrimination of all kinds. The practice of homosexuality was in most places against the law, and thus it was little stretch to suggest that those who engaged in "criminal" conduct had no rights at all. Acts of discrimination against homosexuals generated a supportive public response, even, one presumes, from closet homosexuals, who had to appear to adopt popular prejudices to hide their life-styles. The straight community remains ambivalent about a number of symbolic issues but came gradually to believe that homosexuals were as capable on the job as straight people and were therefore entitled to equal opportunities in the workplace.

What all of these controversies about the ends of political life share is a distinctive life history. At first, there is near unanimous support for the values and beliefs of the old order. Then comes a period of value change, where people rethink previous views (and some of those people are replaced by a newer generation not rooted in the old order), which leads finally to a new quasi-consensus on equality. If we could witness the whole process, it would resemble an "S" curve: low support for equality, followed by a trend to increasing acceptance of rights, followed by a leveling out at a new higher level of belief in equality. We don't get to witness the full process, because the period before social change and the period after the new consensus produce no measures. Only when the

---

[9] This gives short shrift to the suffragette movement and to other agitations for better treatment. But it remains the case that acceptance of unequal treatment of various kinds was all but universal in the early 1960s.

controversy is "live" do survey organizations pose questions about it. That means that what's left is the trend portion of the "S," the time of steadily growing support for equality.

We have measures for each of the three cases. None by itself is ideal, for only a minute portion of the survey experience is directed to issues of ends. In the racial case, for example, many national samples of respondents have answered numerous questions, almost all of which concerned government actions. But for the racial case, one item in the University of Michigan National Election Studies posed the simple question, "Are you in favor of desegregation, strict segregation, or something in between?"[10] For the case of women's roles, we have the following: "Recently there has been a lot of talk about women's rights. Some people feel that women should have an equal role with men in running business, industry, and government. Others feel that a woman's place is in the home." This is followed by a probe, posed in varying manners, which asks the respondent to position him- or herself somewhere on or between the two positions. And in the gay rights issue we have, "In general, do you think homosexuals should or should not have equal rights in terms of job opportunities?"

What all of these have in common is that they pose questions about preferred outcomes, making no reference to policies or actions that might produce the outcomes. What they also have in common is trend, a pattern that turns out to be quite rare elsewhere. Each of the little series in Figure 2.1 trends upward. Each shows no sign of reversal, other than year-to-year zigs and zags probably attributable to sampling fluctuation, the minor misestimation in each survey due to the role of chance in sample selection. The process that would produce such trending is permanent opinion change. In the case, for example, of women's roles, the data are consistent with a story in which people hold a variety of views when the issue emerges into public discussion, and then a systematic process is begun in which numerous people change from the traditional belief – gender discrimination is normal, natural, and acceptable – to the new one – that women are people and that all people deserve equal treatment. This opinion change on value issues tends to have a "trap-door" character; movement occurs in one direction only.[11]

[10] I construct a summary scale from analysis of each of the three possible choices over time.
[11] A slightly more complicated story would add a second process. Some people probably retain their traditional views but discover that it is now socially unacceptable (i.e., "politically incorrect") to express their true views on the subject. So long as the rules of political correctness do not change, this "apparent" change would also be permanent. The intriguing possibility is that both sincere change and insincere expression of politically correct

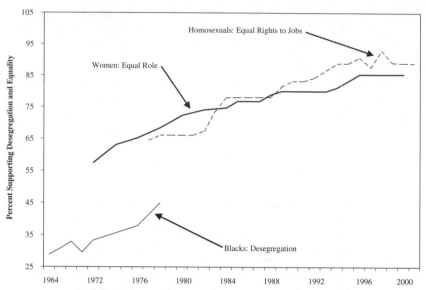

FIGURE 2.1. Support for desegregation (blacks), equal roles (women), and equal job rights (homosexuals), 1964 to 2001.

Our sister discipline, sociology, has produced a good deal of evidence of trending changes of this character. On issues such as those we have examined, as well as attitudes toward family, sexual behavior, and the like (Davis and Smith 1980; Smith 1981, 1990), cultural change produces trends in attitudes: Things move only in one direction. Trends of such character are so rare in political science (these three cases nearly exhaust the evidence!) that we have an obvious need of an explanation. Why is it in things political that attitudes reverse over time?

How is the polity different from the society? The key difference is this: Governments respond. If public opinion changes, governments do not stand idly by and observe. When their future depends on being in line with public opinion, they adapt. What is distinctive about political, as opposed to sociological, questions is that they are about what government should do. If what governments do changes in response to opinion change, then the stimulus to public opinion itself is not constant.

Return to Wlezien's thermostat analogy. Imagine that our citizens are residents of a household where the thermostat is set to the average preference for heat. Then as many will prefer "warmer" as prefer "cooler."

views would probably have the same effect in the long run, producing a society in which only one position is publicly expressed and producing genuine conformity among new generations exposed to the now unified norm.

But imagine now that for some reason the preferences change (while the setting does not), so that majority sentiment favors "warmer" over "cooler." Politics differs from the thermostat because government, which wishes to be popular, will sense the change in majority sentiment and move to a warmer setting to appeal to it. Having done so, it will change the sentiment back toward a neutral level. The majority that wanted "warmer" got "warmer," and now only smaller numbers of heat extremists will insist on "warmer" still. The consequence, if government is adaptive in this sense, is that no policy preference will ever trend permanently in one direction. The trend, which pulls government action along with it, is inherently self-defeating. The prediction from this little responsiveness theory is that all public opinion about policy preferences will move back and forth over time. That, we see below, is decidedly the case.

WHAT ARE THE CONSIDERATIONS?: POLICY DOMAINS

Interviewers pose queries. Respondents think about considerations, general sorts of beliefs that might help to answer the queries. What are those considerations? We don't know. One way to learn is to work backward, to use the evidence of what people say in response to specific questions to put together a kind of puzzle in which we can work the evidence until it points to the unseen suspect lurking behind the scenes, as in a detective story.

The idea that people think differently about different sorts of policies serves as a starting point. We don't know that it is true, but most people believe that the sort of attitudes one brings, for example, to the question of whether there should be a waiting period for the purchase of handguns would be something quite different from whether or not we should spend more to improve highways.

I proceed along this path – dividing the topic of what people want government to do into agreed on policy domains – also to organize a description of the contours of American public opinion. Part of my motivation here is that what I read and hear in media reports and in personal conversations leads me to believe that we don't have a very good sense of the most fundamental questions about public opinion. For example, are people liberal, moderate, or conservative, on average? One can hear factual claims that each is true from professional observers of politics, sometimes all three claims in the same day. Or, is the public mainly for or against government spending?

We don't have agreement on answers to these questions partly because we are overwhelmed with the evidence. We have thousands of survey reports of what people want from government. But they do not add up to a fixed impression of what the animal looks like. And it isn't just the details we lack. We don't know whether it has tusks or scales, whether it walks, flies, or slithers. Each of those survey reports answers part of the question, but only in terms of the words of the question. And the particular words are a problem. Different words produce different answers.

Generous Americans say they want government to do more to help poor people. But they draw the line at "welfare." Which one of these is right? Which really captures American public opinion (see Smith 1987)? Given a choice between spending more or less, almost across the board majorities want government to spend more. And majorities also say that their taxes are too high. Which one of these is right? The one that says Americans are basically liberal or the one that says they are basically conservative?

The situation isn't desperate. All that evidence should answer the questions. But what it requires is getting beyond the specific words, getting a general idea of the ebb and flow of opinion that does not depend on particular questions and particular words. That is the task of the section of this chapter to come. I take up one policy domain at a time and describe the controversies, the state of opinions in the domain, and their trends. At the end, I turn again to the question of What are the considerations? using the evidence of the tour for a beginning of an answer. I start with the bundle of issues called the "welfare state," the controversies and opinions about how much government should do in domestic affairs that at most times is the basic conflict of American politics.

The New Deal Welfare State

Conflicts about how big the government should be and how much it should do are the staple division of the American political parties, a state of affairs that dates to Franklin Roosevelt's New Deal. Not all of these controversies have such a long history. Federal aid to education came along more than twenty years after the New Deal; racial controversies date mainly from the early 1960s; and federal environmental policies joined the package around 1970. Each of these policies added to the partisan debate about the appropriate size of government.

Education
Americans like education. They believe in it, want government to spend on it, and are willing to pay taxes to see it done. Given a choice between doing more or less, spending more or less, or taxing more or less in order to spend

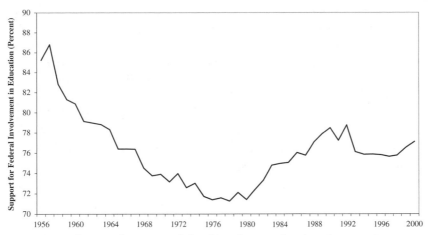

FIGURE 2.2. Support for greater federal involvement in education, 1956 to 2000.

more or less, about three out of four choose more. Other issues, such as
the current debate over vouchers for support of private schools, come and
go, leaving virtually no record of public attitudes. But we have an excellent
record of how Americans feel about expanding the federal role to improve
education. Some seventy-five surveys comprising eight separate series are
available for the span of 1956 to 2000. Because these series are highly
correlated, all telling the same story, the trend over this forty-year span
is easily estimated. A typical query asks respondents whether they want
more, less, or about the same government spending for education.

That trend, seen in Figure 2.2, shows peak support in the earliest years,
when federal support for education was new and heavily debated. That
support slides steadily down toward the 70 percent range on the eve of
Ronald Reagan's 1980 election. Over the span of the twelve Reagan-
Bush years, this support for greater federal involvement rebuilds, to peak
at about the time of Bill Clinton's 1992 election, and then falls off again
after Clinton is in office.

To preview what is to come, this pattern will be seen over and over again
and is clearly not a coincidence. American public opinion systematically
moves contrary to the direction of the party of the White House. Put liberals in charge and opinion grows conservative. Put conservatives in charge
and Americans respond with new liberalism. Why should this be the case?

An explanation begins with some assumptions about where the public
stands relative to the two national political parties. The parties define the
left and right poles of American politics. That is evident in the current era

of polarized ideological parties. It was less evident in the middle years of the twentieth century, when both parties had large factions whose views were out of line with the dominant party stand: conservative southerners in the Democratic Party, liberal northeasterners in the Republican Party. Less true then than now, it was still the case that the parties on average defined left and right.

Where public opinion lies is often contentious in political rhetoric, where we regularly fight about where "true" or "real" (or "silent") majorities lie in American politics. In fact, the rhetoric is silly. The American public is moderate (relative to the parties). That is almost necessarily true; having both parties line up to the left or right of public opinion would require both to forgo the goal of winning elections by taking stands known to be unpopular. But it isn't *only* a truism. To live on a daily basis with the raw materials of what the public thinks and prefers is to be impressed over and over again that middle is more appealing to more people than is the left or right. That is true absolutely, not only relative to the parties.

Now think about what the public wants and what it gets from government. It wants the middle road but has to choose in elections between a party of the right and one of the left. Thus it is not coincidence that it is on average dissatisfied by what it gets. It wants moderate and it gets conservative from Reagan and Bush. It responds by expressing more liberal views when government is conservative. It wants moderate and it gets liberal from Bill Clinton. It responds by becoming more conservative. All we have to do is forget the rhetoric that claims the voters really want far left or far right outcomes – those views are represented by the atypical people who write letters to the editor and call in on talk radio – and the response is exactly what we would expect.

Health Care

The impetus to expand the American welfare state failed before it got to health care. Unlike other industrial democracies, the United States on various occasions considered extending health benefits to its citizens as a right but backed away. But public opinion on the matter suggests that fundamental support for greater government efforts in this direction has always existed. Although it lacks the near unanimity of support seen in the education case, hefty majorities have always supported doing more. ("Doing more," of course, may be considerably less than adopting a national health care program.)

Truncating the graph of Figure 2.3 at the 1992 election of Bill Clinton would show a trend toward rising support for federal action that would

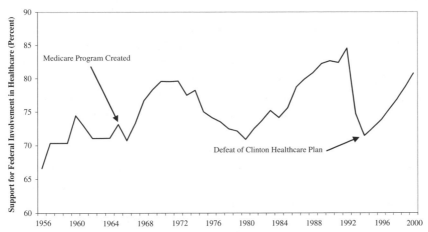

FIGURE 2.3. Support for greater federal involvement in health care, 1956 to 2000.

easily have supported a fundamental change in the system. The reality, we all know, was otherwise. Once an actual program was proposed and debated, that support fell dramatically. The story often told – that the Clinton plan was defeated by intensive lobbying, with an accompanying public relations campaign, of the insurance industry – might have some truth. But I think that what we know about public opinion may say more. Why can a near consensus exist in the election year – about 85 percent of all those taking a stand advocated more government action – and support wither a year and a half later as the matter moved through Congress?

One of the things we know about public opinion is that the public doesn't approach public policy issues in the style of the policy analyst. The analyst asks, "What are the costs and what are the benefits, and does the latter exceed the former?" The public asks, "What are the benefits?" (and perhaps, "Will someone pay taxes for them?") Thus, many proposals for government action garner majority support, but majority support that does *not* predict continuing support if something is actually done.

In the health care case, the benefit, universal coverage, was truly popular. But what the surveys couldn't assess was how many citizens were willing to give up some of the quality and access to health care that they currently enjoyed in order to gain this benefit for somebody else. The debate over the Clinton plan gave us more than Harry and Louise, the famous fictional pair who talked about their diminished options in TV ads. It also gave the public an education about the immense complexity of the patchwork of arrangements for provision of health coverage. A key part of that education was coming to understand that a national plan would involve costs to people, that it could not raise some to a satisfactory level and leave others untouched, that it had to lower the benefits some received in order to raise those of others. There is much debate about the defeat of the Clinton plan, much of it focused on the skill, or lack thereof, of scheduling the issue, the role of the insurance industry, and so forth. I am inclined to the simpler view that the plan failed because, despite widespread support for reform, when people found out that the cost would include diminished access to health care for themselves, they were unwilling to pay it. I believe, that is, that the support was genuine but just not great enough to induce willingness to pay the personal cost.

But the matter needs some perspective. Even while the Clinton plan was going down to defeat, there was long-term support for government doing more. And what we have witnessed since that debate was settled in 1994 is a return to public concern over health care and support for government action. Congress responded in more incremental policies, health care portability and the continuing debate over a HMO "Bill of Rights," both of which draw strong public support. Before 1994 public opinion recognized a growing problem of increasing numbers left uninsured when employers declined to provide benefits. That problem continued to grow after the defeat of the Clinton plan. So did support for government action.

Cities
Most Americans live in or near cities. Even those large numbers of people who choose to live well outside city limits deal with the cities and their problems and find the quality of their lives affected by urban problems. If the housing stock is in decay or mass transit is ineffective, even the suburbanites who have escaped urban problems are affected. Metro areas have a core, and it is hard for life to be good in the periphery if things are troubled at the core. Thus, we have a long history of policy questions about how the government in Washington can aid the often financially troubled central cities. If it were only the residents of central cities who cared about such problems, we could predict very little support for federal action. Instead, about 60 percent of all Americans over time support proposals for federal action against urban problems.

The intriguing thing about this issue domain is that the opinion is unmatched to a lively public debate in Washington. In the years since the urban renewal programs of the 1950s, there has not been a continuing debate, as there always is in education, in health care, in environment, in welfare, and in a host of other areas. Public opinion supports government action but only piecemeal actions – grants for sewer treatment, mass transit, and the like – get debated, and not very much at that. We know that our central cities are not for the most part very desirable places to live and we would like them to be. Given a tax structure that leaves cities chronically unable to raise the revenue needed for improvements, the federal government is the logical source of action. But it is a policy domain with few proposals, none of which is centrally important to American politics.

The public opinion data reflect the absence of a vigorous debate. Because there is no continuing central controversy, there is no basis for a focused public opinion and no good questions for surveyors of opinion to ask. Consequently, treatment of urban issues is scattered and limited as compared with policy domains that sustain continuing debates. The span of time for which we can assess support for government action to aid cities is 1965 to 2000 (see Fig. 2.4). The data consist of fifty-six items comprising four series.

Thus the trends we can see in Figure 2.4 aren't as clear as others. Although we lack a "before" condition that would have made better evidence, the low points in 1965–66 are probably a response to the terrible urban riots of those years. Coverage of the riots in city after city painted a starkly unsympathetic portrait of the urban poor as looters and burners. Like other series, the urban aid issue is at a relative conservative high at the time of the Reagan election and rebounds to liberalism in 1992.

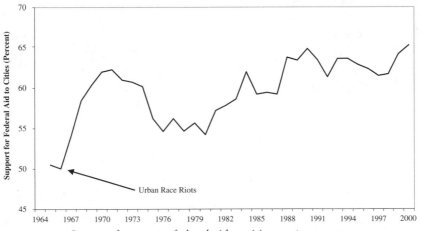

FIGURE 2.4. Support for greater federal aid to cities, 1965 to 2000.

The appearance of an upward trend over the final twenty years probably reflects the absence of a debate. Respondents, not presented with an actual program for urban action, find it easy to endorse action. In the absence of a real proposal, "doing more" can seem to be a cost-free benefit.

Environment

Before 1970 the environment was the concern of scientists, conservationists, hunters, and lovers of nature. But it was not an issue in American politics. It became one overnight with the surge of environmental awareness that emerged in the early 1970s. The issue's thirty-year history is one of solid public consensus on doing more. That was easy to understand in the earliest years of environmental controversy, for then the issue was regulation of polluters, and that really meant, in the early formulation, industrial polluters. Since the public got the benefit and someone else paid the cost, public support came easily.

After the early experience it might have been expected that we would face tougher issues. When obvious industrial pollution was regulated, we would then begin to confront the tougher choices. If environmental degradation could not be controlled without eliminating the base of our prosperity, then we would balance environment against prosperity and draw the line somewhere. Or so it seemed. Because in truth there are painful trade-offs. But public opinion was unwavering. The public wanted and still wants environmental improvement, and it wanted it regardless of trade-offs. That's what the data show.

Because real trade-offs exist and national policy must deal in them, it does. Issues such as standards for allowable trace pollutants or gasoline mileage requirements get processed in a give and take of technical and economic discussion. Compromises are made. But no one openly confronts the public's zeal for a clean environment. Ronald Reagan came as close as anyone in his 1980 stump speech about "getting government off your back." Insiders understood that to mean relaxing environmental regulation of business. The public probably did not understand it that way, and Reagan would have been wise in not wanting it to.

Given a choice between doing more about the environment and anything else, the environment wins. A Gallup question asks:

With which one of these statements about the environment and the economy do you most agree? Protection of the environment should be given priority, even at the risk of curbing economic growth. Or, Economic growth should be given priority, even if the environment suffers to some extent.

FIGURE 2.5. Support for pro-environment policies, 1956 to 2000.

This formulation forces a confrontation between cherished goals. Even here, when the cost is front and center, twice as many give priority to the environment over economic growth. On easier issues, such as whether the government should do more and spend more, the environmental consensus is larger.

My emphasis on consensus here should not be taken to say that there is no movement in environmental attitudes. There is. It is just that the range of movement is between 70 percent support for doing more at the bottom (see Fig. 2.5) and almost 90 percent at the top. The timing of these highs and lows is what we have come to expect. Environmental conservatism rises over the 1970s and peaks in 1980, returning to liberalism over the course of the Reagan and Bush administrations. Along with other components of the welfare state, support drops off as the activist Bill Clinton takes office.

Race

Much has been written about racial attitudes. Unlike views about, say, education or environment, we have a public debate not only on racial issues themselves, but even about what attitudes toward race are (see Schuman, Steeh, and Bobo 1985). Because the topic commands popular interest, much that is written is "pop," and much of that is adversarial, arguing that Americans are or are not racists. So, simple description is a challenge.

Part of the challenge is the discrepancy, already noted, between attitudes toward outcomes and attitudes toward policy, the means to outcomes. Americans say they want racial equality. And I think they mostly mean it.[12] But the policies that might achieve the equality goal – front and center affirmative action hiring or college admission programs – are among the most controversial of all policy debates. That, I think, should not surprise us as much as it does. Affirmative action – the kind with teeth that actually produces results – is inherently controversial. It involves taking something valued away from somebody to give it to somebody else. We should expect government "taking away" to be controversial. Popular policies such as education and environment involve lifting the standard for everybody. If, for example, giving a good education to one person had to come at the expense of taking it away from another, then education, too, would be controversial.

Part of the affirmative action controversy hangs on the distinction between righting old wrongs, which generally draws support, and extending preference to black Americans because of the generic wrong of slavery and discrimination to the black population. Where preference compensates for specific wrongdoing, it draws some support. In a question posed by the National Election Studies about companies with a history of discrimination, about even numbers favor or oppose preferential hiring. When the issue is posed generically in the same surveys as simply "past discrimination," only about 15 percent support preferential hiring. An inference about true racial attitudes based on one of these questions would clearly fail to predict the other.

Much more than in other controversies, racial policy attitudes are unsettled. Different aspects of the racial agenda do not display similar movements over time. Thus, our summary measure needs to be treated with more than usual caution. It could change, even fairly dramatically, if the relative mix of policy questions about race were to change. The appearance of a trend toward liberalism in the long haul is a trend in overall expression of support for greater government involvement and activity. It does not imply a greater willingness for measures to overcome the effects of past discrimination on the whole population.

With that caveat in mind, Figure 2.6 shows some of the cycling behavior seen elsewhere. Racial attitudes were highly responsive in the peak

---

[12] I state this as a belief, rather than a fact, because we have little evidence on the matter. Most attitude questions focus on policies, not outcomes. And expressions of belief in equality mix real belief with politically correct expression to an unknown degree.

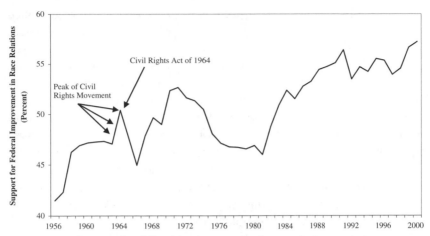

FIGURE 2.6. Support for federal improvement of race relations, 1956 to 2000.

years of the civil rights movement. Generally following the movement, the rightward turn in 1966, called "backlash" at the time, is a probable reaction to the urban race riots of 1965–66. Whatever it is that Americans truly want government to do about race, they clearly wanted less of it in the period that ushered Ronald Reagan into the White House. And they came to want more of it when policy shifted rightward (down in Fig. 2.6).[13] And then they wanted only a bit less after Bill Clinton gave them more. The racial series, however, is unusual in rising to a liberal peak at the end of the Clinton presidency.

Welfare

Welfare, in the questions posed, is all about money. In the public mind, however, its image is inextricably linked also to race. It is a working routine of journalism always to tie abstract stories about policy to the experiences of particular people. It seems to be a rule in the case of welfare policy always to portray those real recipients as African-American (Gilens 2000).

Welfare, an abstract concept, as used in American politics really means the Aid for Families with Dependent Children (AFDC) program.[14] That's what politicians mean when they use the word and that's what public opinion responds to. "Welfare," thus defined, has a terrible reputation.

---

[13] The Reagan-Bush years are devoid of notable policy proclamations on race. Although neither man was considered a friend of black America, the support for racial equality of the time would have precluded open advocacy of rolling back the clock.

[14] It is now Temporary Assistance for Needy Families (TANF).

A traditional whipping boy for politicians of the right, it is not defended
by the left. "Ending welfare as we know it" was an applause line for
the liberal Bill Clinton. It would be surprising if such an often-abused
program drew much public support, and it does not. Of all the creations
of the Democratic welfare state, it is consistently the least popular. It is the
only such program that regularly draws more opposition than support.

Basic lack of sympathy for the misfortunate would be a natural line of
explanation for the persistent unpopularity of welfare. But that doesn't
square with the evidence. About 55 percent of respondents in the General
Social Survey over time want government to do more, rather than less,
"to improve the standard of living of all poor Americans." Of those who
take a position, one way or the other, heavy majorities want government
to spend more to "aid poor people" in the National Election Studies.

The AFDC program is something different from merely aid to poor
people. It carries a black connotation, in part. And even without that it
would be unpopular. Its numerous opponents claim that it is ineffective,
that it generates dependence, that it creates a culture of permanent, multi-
generation welfare, and that it is widely abused. It has no defenders. That
is best seen in this contrast: About 83 percent of those surveyed in the two
most recent presidential election years want government to spend more
to aid poor people. When the same respondents are asked about spending
on "welfare," support drops to 23 percent.

All this unpopularity aside, trends in welfare attitudes (see Fig. 2.7)
look like the trends we have seen elsewhere. They just move in a lower

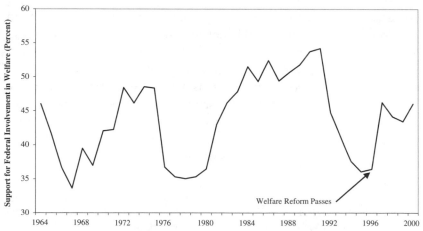

FIGURE 2.7. Support for greater federal involvement in welfare, 1956 to 2000.

range of support. Welfare attitudes are liberal in the 1960s, conservative in the late 1970 and early 1980s, liberal again before Clinton, and conservative after. The one movement that is probably specific to the welfare domain is the increased popularity of welfare spending (always speaking relatively) after the substantial reforms of 1996.

Taxes

Most of what is said about attitudes toward taxes in American politics is based on assumptions, not facts. There is no reason to think taxes should ever be popular. They are pure cost, no benefit. So we do assume that taxation is deeply disliked, that taxpayers are angry much of the time, occasionally in revolt. What we know of the fact of tax attitudes comes mainly from a single series (supplemented here and there by others). On a regular basis since 1947 the Gallup organization has asked: "Do you consider the amount of federal income tax which you have to pay as too high, about right, or too low?"

The lore of the angry taxpayer would suggest near unanimity in the "too high" response. The data are more interesting. Without surprise, not many (usually about 1%) make the extraordinary claim that their tax burden is "too low." The middle response, "about right," I'll call tax tolerance, treating the issue as an implicit dichotomy, "too high" or "not too high."

Over the span of half a century slightly more than a third of all respondents (37%) who were asked this question opt for the tolerant "about right." That, to be sure, is not majority support, but is a good deal more tolerant than the image of angry taxpayers would suggest.

The response to taxation in Figure 2.8 shows the bubble of liberalism for which the 1960s became famous. It has not been seen much in earlier series. Partly, that is just a data problem. Many series began in the late 1960s, and it was in the early 1960s (and even late 1950s) when liberalism was most in evidence.[15] The tax tolerance series captures the full effect, beginning to end. We can also see from the figure what appears to be growing tolerance of the income tax after the Reagan tax cut of 1981. Had we not seen that same increase in liberalism in every other series,

---

[15] The cultural image of the 1960s – flower children, long hair, and ragged dress – is very much an image of the late 1960s. These and many other data suggest that political liberalism was in decline long before the cultural revolt of youth created the image that stamps the decade. The war in Vietnam, which helped to end political liberalism and contributed to the youth revolt, is the dividing line.

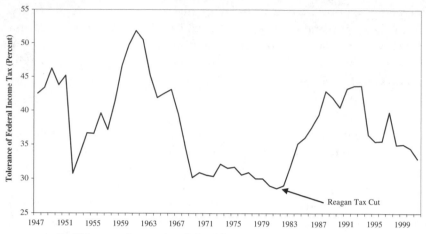

FIGURE 2.8. Tolerance for paying federal income taxes, 1947 to 2001.

it would be easy to interpret it as cause and effect; after the cut, fewer people said taxes were too high.

Seven Issue Domains or One?

It should be coming clear by now that some of the variation in each policy domain that we have attributed to events and conditions in that domain is really something more general. Not education, health care, environment, cities, race, welfare, or taxes, it is a response to the idea of government involvement in this set of domestic controversies itself. Something must account for the common trends across these diverse areas.

To get a sense of how much is general and how much is specific, I put them all together in one graph in Figure 2.9.[16] That gives us the visual opportunity to observe whether they seem to move together or separately.

What impresses me is how little of each domain is independent of the general trend. We can see that racial attitudes have a little trend toward liberalism not shared with the others and that education and tax attitudes were more liberal at the beginning of the 1960s than were the others.[17] A

---

[16] To cram them all together when education and environment are popular and welfare and taxes unpopular, I standardize the data to the common average across all areas (and also the common standard deviation).

[17] The quality and frequency of measures in the first decade or so are considerably less than they later became, and so simple unreliability is another explanation of early differences.

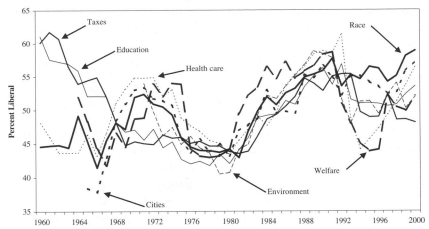

FIGURE 2.9. Issue dynamics of the welfare state: seven domestic issue domains collapsed together.

reaction to urban race riots induces some conservatism to the mid-1960s in race and cities. But after that, the seven different domains behave as if they were just seven different measures of the same thing.

It is not the case that every policy arena behaves the same as every other. As we get away from the New Deal, Fair Deal, New Frontier, and Great Society welfare states, the main line of cleavage between the two parties for this whole period, then some specific and idiosyncratic trends can be found. That is the remaining task of this chapter.

SOME NEWER POLICY CONFLICTS

Unlike education, racial, and environmental policies, which came along later but fit comfortably into the party issue alignment of the times, there are newer issues in American politics that more clearly are something different, not a residue of familiar debates over similar things. I examine three of these here: gun control, the death penalty, and abortion.

Gun Control

The gun control controversy, a staple of American politics since at least the assassination of John F. Kennedy, is wholly different from the standard domestic conflicts. Having little to do with the scope of government and not about spending priorities, it is a matter of regulation on its surface and of symbols beneath its surface. It pits the interest in safety of urban residents against the defense of a symbol of rural life. When the struggle is over handguns, which lack a purpose in the rural setting, then the issue becomes more the control of cherished symbols and equally the right of government to take away what any citizen values.

The politics of gun control is a classic example of an issue that pits a lukewarm majority against a passionate minority. Most Americans support some control of guns, particularly handguns. So long as proposals involve matters of convenience, registration, waiting periods for purchase, and so forth, majorities regularly support controls. But the important political limitation of the "control" side of the issue is that supporters don't make this issue a priority. It appears well down on the list of things that most people care about, far enough down to be forgotten. The gun control opponents, in contrast, feel threatened and are passionate in the face of that threat. Often people with little interest in politics, they are willing to make this one issue the basis for their votes. Thus the gun control issue regularly works for the outnumbered control opponents and, in recent years, Republicans.

The strongest gun control proposal, an outright ban on handgun sales, draws the least support, a near majority (about 44%). Milder measures nearly double that. General propositions about making gun control more or less strict elicit about 90 percent support for the more strict to every 10 percent for the opposite. More than in other areas, trends in gun control are difficult to discern. In part that reflects the changing agenda of the issue. Handguns, "Saturday night specials" (cheap handguns), assault rifles, waiting periods for gun purchase, sales at gun shows – the focus of debate keeps changing. We can see in Figure 2.10 the outlines of trends similar to those of welfare state issues: liberalism in the 1960s, conservatism in the early 1980s, and rebounding liberalism. But some of the wrinkles are different.

The Death Penalty

Capital punishment was very nearly abolished in the United States in the 1970s. It survived because the American public wanted it. After a decade of disuse, in which the states repaired their laws, but none seemed to want to be the first to restart executions, it was triggered finally because one man, convicted murderer Gary Gilmore, demanded his right to be executed under the law. After a history in which capital punishment was a basic part of the American criminal justice system and enjoyed wide

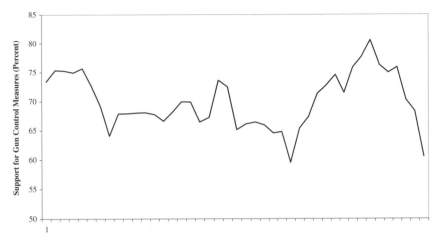

FIGURE 2.10. Support for stricter gun control.

public support, the Supreme Court in the 1960s laid a foundation for what looked at the time to be a likely abolition. The Court found massive irregularities in the way that the death penalty was applied, objecting particularly to near universal laws that gave the life and death decision to the jury. Because white juries in the South routinely imposed the death sentence on black defendants and spared whites charged with similar crimes, the Court held that the death sentence, although not inherently counter to the U.S. Constitution, was applied in a manner that was unconstitutional. What ensued was a ten-year period in which no person was executed in the United States. Had that gone on much longer, the passage of time is likely to have tipped the death penalty into unconstitutional status under the prohibition against cruel and unusual punishments. Defining "cruel" is difficult, but a punishment never imposed for over a decade does begin to look "unusual."

When the Court thus struck down state laws, virtually all of them, public opinion on the matter came into play. The states might have taken the hint that the Court was troubled with the death penalty and let it slide. Instead, and in part because of public support, almost all of them promptly set about to revise their laws, eliminating the jury discretion to which the Court most objected. Thus when Gilmore demanded to be executed, the laws of Utah and other states met the letter of the Court's intent, and execution began again.

There has always been majority support for the death penalty. The highest level of opposition to it occurred when it was often applied in a

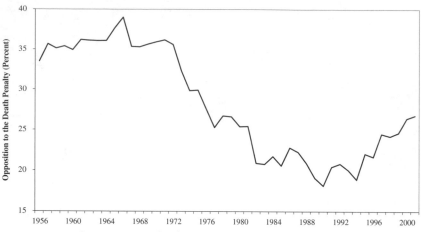

FIGURE 2.11. Opposition to the death penalty.

discriminatory manner and more or less at the same time that courts were troubled by these issues (see Fig. 2.11). That opposition faded on reports of ever-growing violence in America. Some of these were true, particularly in the 1970s and early 1980s. After that, crime receded, but the reports of crime did not. At about the same time that violent crime was receding, local TV stations all over the United States were discovering that an "all-crime" format was a sure thing for ratings success. Abandoning local focus, thousands of TV stations began covering every sensational crime in the country. Thus, TV viewers were exposed to a level of gruesome violence none had ever before experienced. Driven by media-induced fear of crime, support for the most permanent of solutions increased.

The upswing in opposition to the death penalty – still not very large – occurred in the context of multiple reports (often based on DNA reanalysis) that innocent people had been executed. State governors, who usually have to sign off personally on executions, began to show some reluctance to do so in several instances. That is where we stand. The death penalty is popular and is employed – in some places on a very large scale – and the debate will continue.

Abortion

The abortion issue has a starring role in the next chapter on issue alignments. So I won't say everything I have to say here. Given all the heat associated with the pro-choice versus pro-life war of words in national politics, it is useful to approach the issue with a calm description of the basic facts of public opinion. My tool for doing so is the almost thirty-year span of the General Social Survey (GSS), which in most years presents respondents with a battery of seven questions, each asking whether abortion should be legal under stated circumstances. The lead-in to the question, "Please tell me whether or not you think it should be possible for a pregnant woman to obtain a legal abortion if..." is the same for all. Then respondents get a description of circumstances, for example, "the family has a very low income and cannot afford any more children."

The answers to these queries, a thirty-year average for each, begin to outline basic opinion on the matter. They are presented in bar graph form in Figure 2.12. In each case, what is presented is the percent agreeing that abortion should be legal.

Given about 3 percent "don't know" responses, then most of those who don't endorse legal abortion are opposing it. The question that defines the full pro-choice position is the first one, that abortion should be legal if the woman wants one for any reason. So about 40 percent of Americans are fully pro-choice by this criterion. Saying no under all conditions is the full pro-life stance. That is defined by those who say no to the most popular exception, the health of the woman. That averages about 10 percent.

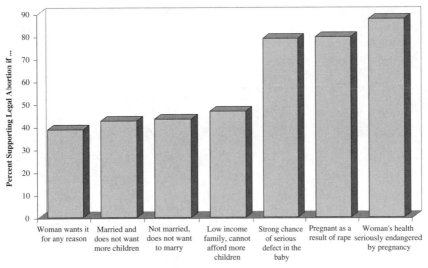

FIGURE 2.12. General Social Survey respondents who would allow legal abortion under various circumstances, 1973 to 2000.

These numbers basically assert a pro-choice dominance. But the data tell another story too. The conditions that occur most commonly, variations on unwanted pregnancy due to life circumstance, get very little sympathy from the GSS respondents. They add only a very minor increment to the 40 percent in favor of abortion on demand. The conditions that produce big numbers supporting legal choice are relatively rare ones. Most women seeking abortions will not present a high probability of defects to the child, are not victims of rape, and do not have a serious threat to their health from pregnancy. Consequently, the numbers can be read to assert some discomfort with the status quo, which is abortion on demand (at least if providers exist and are willing.)

It is also notable, given the white-hot portrayal of this debate in the press, that about half of all Americans take a moderate, in between, position on the issue. Endorsing neither absolute choice nor any absolute right to life, they support choice based on circumstances, sometimes in favor of it, sometimes not.

It is difficult to make sense of trends in abortion attitudes. Looking at essentially the same data as in Figure 2.13 through 1990, I once wrote (Stimson 1991) that the abortion trend was a flat line. That is no longer true. What appears to be the case is that abortion attitudes are beginning to align with the standard left-right debate that I have called the welfare state. Totally cross-cutting at the outset, increasingly those who are liberal on domestic issues generally are also pro-choice on abortion; those who are conservative are also at the pro-life pole. Arbitrarily cutting the trend

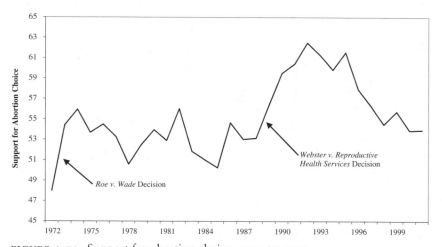

FIGURE 2.13. Support for abortion choice, 1972 to 2001.

line at about 1990, we can say that there is no trend in the first segment, followed by trends that look a lot like trends in other issue domains following that.[18] I revisit the changing alignment issue in Chapter 3.

These ten issue domains nearly exhaust the possibilities for domestic issue controversies on which there is a sufficiently rich record that we can view a life history. That is not to say that these are the only issues that matter. There is a long list of others that may have played some role in our politics – school prayer and vouchers for private education, to name two – but they lack the lengthy span and history of survey queries that mark these issues.

We are left to wonder how, if at all, they fit together. Answering that question is the business of Chapter 3. It begins with a theory of issue connections.

---

[18] The appearance of dramatic movement after 1990 is, however, largely illusion. The range of variation of the series is so slight that any movement looks big. A figure that used the full possible range of 0 to 100 would show shifts just barely discernible.

3

Left and Right Movements in Preference

In 1972, a year before the famous *Roe v. Wade* Supreme Court decision on abortion, a woman seeking a therapeutic abortion faced a much different situation. Abortion was illegal in nearly all jurisdictions. But one state at a time, things were changing. State legislatures were liberalizing the law to recognize the reality of medical practice at the time. Women were having safe legal abortions because doctors supported their decisions and, to skirt the law, were willing to call the procedure something else.

When the states acted they faced organized opposition from the Roman Catholic Church.[1] On the other side were physicians and old-line organizations supporting family planning such as Planned Parenthood, then not a great deal more controversial than the Girl Scouts. The public support for abortion liberalization we did not know as well as we now do; it was not as controversial as it now is. But it seems clear that large numbers of supporters were women, women who were well educated, played tennis or golf at the club, and voted for the Republican Party. Support for abortion (and family planning generally) came, that is, from the part of America that had higher income, was better educated, and lived in the suburbs. These are descriptions that are roughly accurate also for the Republican Party.

Support for abortion rights in 1972 was not "liberal" and definitely not Democratic. The Democrats were then more solicitous of the views of the Catholic Church, which had long been, if not an ally, the religious home of many of the ethnic voters who were Democrats. Abortion was

---

[1] Southern states, with mostly trivial Catholic populations, were sometimes in the forefront of liberalization.

a medical issue and only secondarily a religious one. The action was in the states, and the issue drew little attention in national politics. The two political parties pretty much ignored it. If we had known in 1972 that abortion would come to divide the parties, a guess that the Republicans would be pro-choice and the Democrats pro-life might have been at least as plausible as the alternative.

When delegates to the Republican National Convention met in August 1972 to renominate Richard Nixon, fully 69 percent of them expressed themselves in favor of abortion rights.[2] These faithful Republicans, the hardest of the hard-core, the purest of the pure, did not see any conflict between freedom from government regulation of abortion rights and the freedom from regulation that was their traditional position toward business and the economy.

Abortion is tangled in religious and constitutional issues. But the great religious traditions were silent in their ancient teachings, and the U.S. Constitution did not address the matter. The reason for both was the same. Abortion, therapeutic abortion, was really new, a creature of the great progress in surgery of the nineteenth and twentieth centuries. When it became safe, and safe relative to pregnancy, it created possibilities that had not previously existed. It created issues for which tradition had no answers.

Abortion created a nightmare for elected politicians. Before *Roe v. Wade* that was not so. One could advocate liberalization in the name of freedom and of public health and face little organized opposition. The political lay of the land favored the *Roe* decision when it was first considered and then when it was handed down. The opposition from the Catholic Church seemed more doctrinaire than passionate. The Church was in a weak position, having chosen to make a great moral stand against family planning of all kinds. Thus the opposition to abortion was embarrassed by association with a position against prevention of pregnancy that most Americans rejected. The numbers showed that even practicing Catholics used birth control at about the same level as did non-Catholics. The decision to control the number of children, driven by economic and cultural aspirations, seemed beyond the reach of religious doctrine. The passionate commitment to defend unborn life came later, from a movement that was sparked by legalization itself. That movement came to be rooted in a religious

---

[2] The 69 percent approved the right to abortion under a wide range of circumstances, not including extreme ones such as rape or incest. Democrats, meeting a few weeks earlier in the same city to nominate George McGovern, took essentially the same position, 76 percent agreeing to the same question. See Layman 2001.

tradition at the other end of the scale, in fundamental and evangelical Protestantism. It came, after abortion became legal and widespread, from people who did not particularly care about preventing pregnancy but did care about ending it.

If abortion attitudes had been aligned with the parties, life would have been easier for politicians. But they were not, and that made the issue dangerous. A misstep over this dangerous fault line could upset otherwise secure calculations. As issues rarely do, this issue tempted voters to cross party lines in both directions to vote their commitment. It could not remain the case that abortion rights would remain the province of Republican women. It did not, and that has colored much of American politics in the decades that followed.

What happens to issues when they arise anew is one of the main topics of this chapter. I explore abortion and others here, trying to figure out how many dimensions of controversy structure Americans' reactions to the parties and what happens when some new issue causes that number to expand. We need a theory of how issues emerge, how they evolve, and how multiple facets of conflict come to be encapsulated in a two-sided struggle between the parties. I begin with theory.

THE ISSUE EVOLUTION THEORY OF ISSUE ALIGNMENT

A large and complex society has immense possibilities for producing conflicts over public policy. Every time a diverse and dynamic economy rubs against the public domain, it generates issues for the public order. In principal the number of public issues is almost boundless. While one might imagine an *administrative* structure that could deal with almost boundless controversies – for example, the whole rule-making and rule-enforcing structure of all the administrative agencies of the federal government – it is hard to imagine a political structure that deals with numerous unrelated issues.[3]

Politics has limits. If we conceive it in democratic terms as a dialog between voters and government, then the channel capacity of that dialog has stark constraints. A citizenry that is mainly not interested in public life – which pretty much has to be the case if that same citizenry is productively employed doing something else – cannot ponder a long list of

---

[3] This argument builds on a joint effort with Ted Carmines in our 1989 book, *Issue Evolution: Race and the Transformation of American Politics*. The theory has been extended to cover the abortion controversy by Greg Adams (1997) and to women's rights by Christina Wolbrecht (2000). Some elements are new in this treatment.

controversies. Legislatures can deal in hundreds of issues at most. There are not enough days in the calendar for thousands or tens of thousands or more.

But more than all these, the central mechanism for deciding public controversies, the election, is an extraordinary issue bottleneck. The number of things that can be talked about in a campaign is small (if that talk has any chance of reaching the voters, who by and large are not listening very carefully.) The number that voters can take into mind in making their voting decision is small. And the tightest constraint of all of these forces is the number of issues that can be decided by the outcome. Although election winners can and do claim that everything they stand for is endorsed by the fact of their win, objective observers, who serve as referees in this process, rarely concede that anything has been decided. It is quite impossible that this channel could carry numerous messages.

This abstraction about candidates, voters, and messages connects to the party system. If the voter's decision is between exactly two parties and their nominees – as it normally is in the United States – then it becomes very hard to imagine how we would settle multiple unrelated controversies with one vote. We could *claim* to have settled them, but for that claim to have reality, it would have to be the case that voters weighed each matter separately, came to a conclusion, and factored all of these influences into the single vote. The problem is that the mechanism of choice – a single vote cast for one of two candidates and parties – does not permit the expression of multiple and conflicting views.

A single vote is binary, a "bit" in information theory. A bit is the smallest possible unit of information. It can carry the summary result of a mix of considerations, but it cannot convey the considerations themselves. Think of voting as a censoring process. You can have independent views on multiple controversies, and if the issues are truly independent, the candidates also will have multiple views on multiple controversies. Consequently, as the number of issues goes beyond, say, two or three, it becomes exceedingly unlikely that either of two candidates will have the same mix that you have. The voting process doesn't allow you to divide your vote in proportion to the number of issues on which you agree, voting, say, two-thirds' vote for candidate A, with whom you agree on two issues, and one-third for B, who lines up with your views on the third. That is the nature of censoring, forcing an expression into a form that may not carry all of the original information.

A multiparty vote also is a censoring process, even a pretty extreme one, but it allows more than a single bit of information. Imagine a standard

European party system that divides along two axes, one left-right, as in the United States, and the other along religious lines, clerical versus secular. Then you can have at least four parties who represent the possible combinations of the two dimensions, left-clerical, left-secular, right-clerical, and right-secular. Choosing one of the four now carries two bits of information about your preferences, how you feel about left versus right *and* how you feel about clerical versus secular.

A lot of ink has been spilled arguing about the superiority of various party systems for allowing the rational expression of voter preferences. That is not my interest. The two-party system appears to be a pretty permanent fact of American politics. I wish to assume that this is the case and then exploit that assumption.

Ask how parties and candidates are affected by the knowledge that a vote in a two-party system can carry preferences along a single dimension of choice, say, left versus right, but not more than one. Candidates and parties want to win elections, not to solve problems in information theory. But as they consider strategies for winning, this issue of information censoring looms in the background. How should they structure a set of positions on issues to present to the voters?

Here it is useful to distinguish between what they say in platforms and what they choose to be the central messages, conveyed over and over again to the voters through the campaign. The platform will mention many issues. Many of these will be what Donald Stokes (1963) referred to as "valence" issues, declarations that the party is in favor of peace, prosperity, good education, stable families, a strong national defense, and on and on. "Valence" issues have the character of appearing to be issues, but actually are assertions of support for values that are nearly universally held. Real issues, what Stokes called "position" issues, are genuine controversies on which numerous reasonable people are found on both sides. Some of those involve benefits for a specialized constituency, whether it be farmers, the textile industry, or whomever. These have the character of being of considerable interest only to those directly affected, not to ordinary voters.

The things candidates talk about on the campaign trail and in candidate debates are the platform that voters see and react to. Candidates talk about many "issues" in the campaign. This, among other things, demonstrates competence, showing that the candidate has thought about public debates and has a thoughtful position on each. But the many "issues" commonly are many cases of the same issue dimension. Democrats promise to do more about education, to give support for farms and cities, to make sure

What happens then? After a critical moment the two-sided politics in America become four-sided. In each party, already aligned along the old dimension, there are two groups, those supporting and those opposing the new party position. Huge numbers of racial liberals in 1964 called themselves Republicans, and, in parallel, huge numbers of racial conservatives were Democrats. The abortion controversy saw the two parties divide into pro-choice and pro-life factions of comparable sizes.

Such a configuration is unstable. It leaves both candidates and voters misaligned with their parties. Misalignment exerts stresses that produce a dynamic resulting, ultimately, in elimination of the stresses by folding the two-fold alignment into one. The story can be told about either candidates or voters. I take up candidates first.

Story 1: Candidates

Each of the parties has tens of thousands of candidates and potential candidates for public office and thousands of other political professionals associated with party activities. They run the gamut from the most visible candidates for U.S. House and Senate down to the proverbial local dog-catcher. (I wonder where there is a remaining jurisdiction in the United States in which dog-catchers are actually elected and what we writers about politics will do if the answer is "no.") A new issue, one hot enough to have strategic advantage, will polarize all these people into three camps, supporters of the new position, opponents, and an in-between group that lacks strong views and previous public commitments to one side or the other.

When a controversial new position is staked out, the "supporters"– those who have already advocated the position – will of course join with enthusiasm. And most of those in between will find it easier and more comfortable to support their party's new stance than to oppose it. The cost of opposition is estrangement from their party, while going along is costless. The opponents, who, in contrast, will have taken public positions – sometimes intense ones, sometimes even winning political support for them – will not go along. For them it is not costless to join their party's position. They might appear inconsistent and unprincipled and might alienate voters they count on for support. (This was the situation on race of New York Republicans – the party of the liberal Nelson Rockefeller – in the 1960s and 1970s. They could not go along with their party's conservative wing in opposing federal intervention to secure civil rights of black Americans without being at war with their own traditions.)

Assuming for convenience that the pro, con, and neutral groups are of about the same size, within months then the party goes from a fifty-fifty split on the new issue to the beginning of a consolidated position as the neutrals join the "pro's" to form the new party core. Those who oppose the new line are now an uncomfortable minority in the party.

A period of awkwardness for the out-of-line faction follows. Not just are they are sitting on their hands when the applause line for the new position comes, they are sometimes working against their party colleagues, forced to ally with the opposition to remain true to their convictions. Chances are that they represent constituencies that support their views, for example, pro-life Democrats representing ethnic Catholic constituencies in the Northeast. Out of line, they cannot aspire to leadership roles in their national party. Although their colleagues understand the awkwardness of the situation, they would still have to oppose those who oppose the party's stand.

The out-of-line opponents nonetheless might hold out, even for a long career in politics. This will particularly be the case if they have electoral support for their position. When they leave office is when things are likely finally to change. Those from their own party who replace them will usually be aligned with the party's new position (often no longer very new). All the things that made it awkward and difficult for their predecessors are reasons that the new candidates will find it advantageous to align with the party. And one need not be cynical. They might align because they believe. Candidates of a new generation that comes along after an issue evolution is in progress get to choose their party. They will not chose one in which their views are misfit.

Story 2: Voters

Voters, too, will divide into pro, con, or neutral. But most will have far less intense preferences than do the professional politicians, and few will have a *public* commitment to a prior position. As compared with the professionals, then, the neutral segment will be far more numerous. Thus, the voters can move to support their party's new position far more easily than can the more rooted professionals in politics. Fewer will be out of line in the immediate aftermath of the critical moment.

Out-of-line voters may feel some discomfort but do not face the practical difficulties of professional politicians. Some will go along with party leaders and adopt the new position as their own. Some will remain with their party and out of line with its new position for a lifetime. New voters will come on the scene without previous loyalties and find it easier to align correctly. They develop support for the party positions, both old and new, in the process of cementing a bond with their party. So, population replacement eventually produces alignment.

Voters then begin to enforce issue discipline on politicians. The mechanism is primary elections. Primary elections have two important characteristics that lead to such a role. One is that turnout is minuscule. Where 20 percent or so of those who could vote actually choose to do so, it will predictably be the 20 percent hard-core. It will be voters who have intense rather than casual issue commitments. It will be those most involved, most informed.

The information environment they face lends itself to enforcing discipline. In general elections the link of issues to party makes it easy to know who stands for what, easy to choose between them. The party label just in itself encapsulates a lot of useful information. Primary elections, in contrast, lack anything comparable. Voters are in a bind, trying to tell the difference between numerous candidates – not just two – who often take positions so similar to one another that it becomes very difficult to pry them apart. That is particularly true on the issues that define party conflict; every candidate in the primary will have nearly identical views, nearly identical records.

Given the difficulty of finding any daylight between candidate positions on the standard issue set, the new issue emerges as the leading possibility for making the voting decision. Republicans in recent rounds of primaries, for example, nearly all advocate small government and major income tax cuts. And the Republican faithful who turn out to vote in primaries pretty uniformly support that message. How then to decide among candidates? Focus necessarily turns to criteria where differences might be found. Abortion in this context can become the chief basis for a vote. If all candidates are about equally conservative on social welfare and size of government issues, then if some are pro-life on abortion and some are pro-choice, the pro-life candidates will be the winners. Even though the abortion issue is a secondary party stand, it thus can become the primary basis of success or failure in the primary.

In this context there is a certain inevitability to the long term. As the party begins to align on a new issue, such as abortion, it is initially difficult for candidates to be out of line. As the evolution proceeds, eventually it becomes nearly impossible to survive in intra-party politics unless aligned with the dominant party position. The primary election mechanism ensures that once started, a new issue commitment will eventually run to completion. A party cannot cast itself in a new direction on an issue that matters and then later cast it off or ignore it. Once this process starts the alignment of voters with issue stands carries the parties along in the direction initially chosen.

On abortion the parties could have ignored the issue, as they did before 1973. The right to choose was an issue, but it was not a partisan issue then. They could have chosen differently from what they did; the Democrats becoming the party of "life" and the Republicans the party of choice. This process is highly path-dependent. Early steps, that is, dictate later ones.

Issue Bundles

When we ask what is consistent with what, there seem always to be some positions that are married to others. So, for example, Republicans who have long advocated small government now advocate major income tax cuts as a means to reduce the size of government. The two positions go together, seem to be logically linked. Young voters who don't know electoral history in this context would be shocked to discover that no one ever combined these two positions in most of the post–New Deal era. For most of that period Republicans advocated fiscal prudence – that is, balanced budgets – and gave no thought to tax cuts (and the one modern income tax cut came from the Democratic Kennedy administration). But once Ronald Reagan adopted the tax cut in his 1980 platform – characterized as "voodoo economics" by primary opponent George Bush – the tax cut came to seem logically linked to core Republican beliefs.

The key idea here is that things "seem" logically linked. But if we use our deductive logic to demonstrate that link, in virtually every case we fail. Things that seem to go together do not in fact have logical connections. The phenomenon of seeming to go together, Converse (1964) long ago pointed out, is more a matter of psychology (what symbols are shared) and social learning (what kinds of ideas are learned together in one's social background). The key thing in both these cases is that our idea of consistency is *learned*. It is something that is not objectively true, but rather socially constructed. We get used to the idea that certain positions are advocated together by the same people at the same times and places and come to believe that they must be logically tied.

If nothing *is* naturally connected, the corollary is that anything can *seem* connected. If liberalism seems to dictate support for abortion choice, for example, it might have been the case, given different circumstances in the early 1970s, that exactly the opposite connection became "logical." Time is a critical factor in this bundling process. The first time one sees two totally separate issue positions advocated by one party or candidate, they seem to be just that: two ideas espoused by one source. But as time passes and those same two ideas are repeatedly advocated together, for example, liberalism and choice, then they come to seem related. As the process runs to ultimate conclusion, we begin to see the two as two facets of the same thing and think that they are inseparable.

Dimensions

With this little theory in hand, we can now ask the question, "How many dimensions does it take to structure the attitudes of American voters?" We have the elements of an answer. We know that a two-party system tends to create a single issue division that is stable over time, that it generates new issues as a predictable response to the needs of otherwise losing parties to shake up the system, and that these new issues gradually become incorporated into the old issue configuration with the passage of time.

The answer to the dimension question is, then, "one plus." The plus is the residue of novel issues that at any given time are still novel, still independent. Although each new issue ultimately becomes incorporated into the main dimension of conflict, new issues come along often enough – say, on the order of every three to five presidential election cycles – and take so long to fully incorporate that the residue is always present. So when we go looking for the glue that holds issue positions together over time, we should expect to find one clean dimension and on top of that some systematic "undissolved particles" of attitude toward the newer conflicts. We will not find the new issues themselves because they are already aligned with the old for many people and cannot now be pried apart.

No Social Dimension

It is common for pundits to divide American politics into economic and social issues, with the implication that they are two and separable. Even if that were once the case (and we can't know because most such commentary is not based on systematic data analyses, hence not subject to disconfirmation), the dynamic of issue evolution should have resolved two into one by now. What I can say is that there is no discernable social dimension in the survey data. There are social issues, but these issues align with the main division of the parties.

I propose to the reader a commonsense test of issue independence. Find an example issue, say, school prayer, "creation science," or gay rights, and ask, can I say which side of the issue is liberal and which is conservative?

If the answer is "Yes," as it is for me, then these issues cannot be independent. They are just pieces of the common issue bundle on which liberals and conservatives regularly disagree.

If the issue evolution theory is correct, what should we expect for evidence? First, if new issue controversies truly are novel, we should be able to date when they were added to the active political agenda. Then we should be able to show that they were not associated with the parties before that date. And then we should be able to show that they become associated over time.

I look here at three lively possibilities – race, women's roles, and abortion – to see whether they track as predicted.

THREE ISSUE EVOLUTIONS

The evidence of an issue evolution will be a new issue that is not associated with the existing alignment of issues to a party and then becomes so. That requires the measurement of a single issue over a long span of time so that we can assess whether or not it is associated with a party. For a criterion of association we have party identification, what respondents say in response to "Generally speaking, do you usually think of yourself as a Democrat, a Republican, an independent, or what?" (strength of identification is measured on a seven-point scale from strong Democrat to strong Republican).

I select one question from the issue domain in question, the chief criterion being that it is posed in identical terms over a long span of time. Then it is a simple matter to observe for each year the correlation of party identification with the issue measure. If things are as simple as the theory – and they nearly are – then we should see no correlation at the outset of a new issue. That means that the issue has nothing to do with the existing alignment, what I mean by "new" in partisan terms.[4] Then we should see that correlation grow over time as the parties begin to align. That growth will be dynamic, that is, a process that once started carries itself along into the future. There is no comparably easy standard for being fully aligned as the zero correlation standard for nonaligned. But if we observe a sequence of years in which the correlation stops growing, we can be fairly

---

[4] Of course, no issue is ever new in the stronger sense of never having been thought of before. If it were, it would not be a question in a survey. Racial controversies, for example, are older than the country. But race was new as a partisan issue in 1964, the first time in modern America that the two parties squared off on opposite sides of the question.

confident that the process has run its course.[5] We can then estimate a smooth underlying model of the issue evolution that best fits this pattern of correlations. I begin with race, the issue for which the theory was first developed.

Case 1: Race

Before 1964 the politics of race was a politics of region, North versus South. Because Democrats came disproportionately from the South, the Republican Party was slightly more liberal on racial matters than the Democrats. In 1964 Barry Goldwater first voted "no" on the Civil Rights Act of 1964 – probably the single most visible act of legislating of the twentieth century – then became the Republican candidate for president, and then used his "no" vote in a vigorous attempt to add the South to the Republican column.[6] Thus began the process, continuing to this day, in which Republicans became the conservative party on race and the Democratic South ceased to exist.

"Evolution" is a critical part of the issue evolution story. The emphasis of this theory is on the process that ensues after such a critical moment, the way in which thousands of candidates and millions of voters begin sorting themselves along new lines. That evolution is seen in Figure 3.1 in the growth of correlations between racial attitudes (here captured by an item about government involvement in desegregating schools) and partisanship over the period from roughly 1964 to 2000. Each bar is a correlation between race and party for a particular year. Negative in the one measurement before the 1964 campaign, we see a modest positive correlation, capturing the immediate effect of adding the racial dimension to party politics, and then an uneven growth over the following election years.

The smooth line drawn through the bars of Figure 3.1 is the best fitting simple model of the issue evolution process.[7] It tracks the process from

---

[5] We can use the New Deal/welfare state controversies as a standard for what a mature alignment would look like. An item on government responsibility for employment – the best available continuous measure that taps the basic welfare state controversies – serves as an indicator of what is possible. Its correlation with party identification averages .28.

[6] And he "succeeded," winning five Deep South states while losing the rest of the nation. See Carmines and Stimson 1989 for a much more detailed and elaborate telling of the racial issue story.

[7] For those who care about the mathematics, the model is a first-order transfer function for an intervention that is scored zero before 1964 and one in 1964 and all subsequent years.

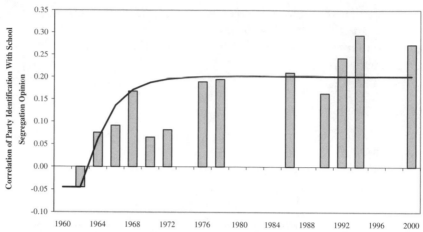

FIGURE 3.1. Correlations between partisanship and school desegregation attitudes: National Election Studies, 1960 to 2000. *Note:* In this figure and Figures 3.2 and 3.3, the vertical axis has a hypothetical range of −1.0 to +1.0, representing the range of possible correlations. The smaller range represents actual observed values. Correlation indicates statistical association. Negative correlation indicates association in the "wrong" direction.

its negative baseline level through a smooth evolution, culminating ultimately in an equilibrium state in which no further alignment occurs. The parameters that determine the shape of the line suggest that the equilibrium was effectively reached by about 1980 and that the process has run its full course.

Case 2: Women

The women's movement of the late 1960s came from outside the party system. With half of all voters at stake, both parties naturally positioned themselves as pro-women. More a cultural than a political phenomenon at the outset, what women wanted from government mainly was a prohibition on the employment discrimination that was then widespread and accepted. Because of a peculiar history, where nondiscrimination by gender had been added to the Civil Rights Act of 1964, almost an afterthought, that battle was won even before the women's movement began to build mass appeal. The movement focused on the more symbolic Equal Rights Amendment. The ERA, first introduced in 1923, had been on the legislative agenda, without any success, for almost fifty years. In that time both political parties routinely endorsed it, but endorsement did not lead to action. When finally adopted by Congress in 1972, the fight was joined. Adopted with a seven-year ratification limit, the ERA fairly quickly was ratified by a majority of states and seemed well on its way to the required three-fourths'. The early success spawned an opposition of people who found the ERA a threat to the traditional order. The opponents, the core of what would eventually become the religious right, moved on the state capitals to reverse the tide. Close to success, the ERA stalled in the late 1970s, when Congress passed a controversial extension of the ratification.

The Republican Party, a traditional ERA supporter, switched sides in its 1980 platform written for the Reagan campaign. Reagan's base, as it had been when he unsuccessfully tried to oust Gerald Ford in 1976, drew heavily from the organized forces of the anti-ERA campaign. Highly visible at the moment, that platform sent a signal that conservatism and feminism would be on opposite sides. Perhaps because of his issue stands and perhaps because of something about Ronald Reagan himself, what ensued was a situation rare in American politics in which candidate and then president Reagan appealed differently to men than to women. Although the difference was not large, it drew attention because we were accustomed to gender not being relevant to politics. The women's movement, which had been largely outside partisan politics, began to see the Reagan administration, and with it the Republican Party, as the enemy of women's rights.[8]

The eight years of the Reagan presidency saw the schism with the women's movement grow. (See the correlations of Figure 3.2. The measure is the "women's role" scale from the National Election Studies, where the poles are "equal roles in running business, industry, and government" and "A woman's place is in the home.") Although Reagan seemed to be gaining at least as much male support as female opposition, his vice president, George H. W. Bush, declared himself "kinder and gentler" in his 1988 campaign. Perhaps for that reason, or maybe it was just coincidence, but the growing polarization by gender attitudes lessened in that year.

The Bush administration witnessed a fight over the "Family and Medical Leave Act," which Bush vetoed. Not gender-specific, it gave rights for unpaid leaves without employer sanctions to "parents." But since

---

[8] Lest the partisan story seem too simple, it is notable that former first lady, Betty Ford, was the honorary chair of the ERA ratification campaign for 1981. Reagan's conservative supporters began the movement away from support for women's rights, but the movement was far from complete in the early 1980s.

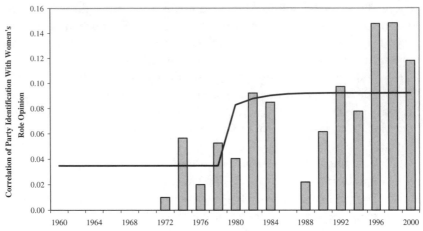

FIGURE 3.2. Correlations between partisanship and women's role attitudes: National Election Studies, 1960 to 2000. *Note:* See Figure 3.1.

most parenting responsibilities fall on women – and child care is a crucial problem in women's struggle for equality in the workplace – the act was seen as a women's issue. Becoming part of the 1992 campaign, Bill Clinton promised to sign such an act and a Democratic Congress promptly passed one in 1993, which Clinton signed. The period after 1988 produced growing evidence of alignment of attitudes toward women and identification with the parties.

We can capture the full process in the model of the effect (the smooth line of Fig. 3.2). In this case we see a very rapid buildup in polarization over the span of the Reagan years, which increases, but only modestly, in the decade after. This case, like the racial case, seems to suggest that the evolution is nearly complete (the model is approaching its estimated equilibrium level). But the fact that the three highest correlations ever are the last three occasions observed suggests that there may still be room for growth.

Case 3: Abortion

Abortion was a state issue before the famous *Roe v. Wade* decision. The trend in the states then was toward liberalization, moving from absolute prohibitions to abortions available when a doctor certified a need for one, usually on psychiatric grounds. Given wide variation in state laws, abortion was good for the travel industry. If the law was restrictive where a woman lived, she could fly somewhere else where it was not. Access to abortion was related to family income. Depending on where you lived, if you could pay the fee, you could find a physician who would declare that pregnancy was a serious threat to the mother. Or, if you had the income, you could bypass the local law to take advantage of a more lenient one somewhere else. The pro-life forces were not yet organized – and with law on their side found little need to organize. *Roe* changed all that.

At the time of *Roe* abortion attitudes were associated with social class. It was middle- and upper-class women who were more likely to assert a right to control their reproductive destinies. Since class is loosely associated with the party system, that meant that Republicans on average were more pro-choice than Democrats.[9] And the author of *Roe*, Justice Harry Blackman, was a Republican, one of Richard Nixon's choices of "strict constructionist" judges to balance the liberalism of the Warren Court.

Unlike the previous cases, race and women's role, there is not a single dramatic event one can point to as the origin of the partisan polarization on abortion. Republicans, in the same conservative 1980 platform that opposed the ERA, proposed a constitutional amendment that would ban abortion. Democrats opposed the ban. But because many Republicans were pro-choice on abortion (most notably, Reagan's vice presidential choice, George Bush[10]) and many Democrats were pro-life, the parties shied away from pushing abortion out front as a campaign issue. But what the parties did not do, individual candidates did. They began to see advantage in pushing their abortion views in primary election contests. Those correctly aligned with their party's views could mobilize the activist primary voters by an appeal on this always emotional issue. In a two-candidate race, taking the correct side on abortion was a winning strategy in both parties. Thus Republicans began to advertise themselves as pro-life while Democrats did the same, pushing choice.

The dynamics of abortion, seen in Figure 3.3, are a little slower than the other cases and appear still incomplete.[11] There are still pro-choice Republicans and pro-life Democrats, but fewer and fewer. Probably we

---

[9] Before *Roe*, the Catholic Church was the only organized force opposing access to abortion. Democrats were slightly more likely to be Catholics than Republicans.

[10] The abortion issue caught all of the Bushs out of line with their party. George H. W. Bush had a pro-choice record in Congress. His wife, Barbara, resisted the pull of party and remained quietly pro-choice while her husband switched sides from necessity. And George W. is reported to have opposed the constitutional amendment to ban abortion in an unsuccessful run for Congress in 1978.

[11] Estimating the issue evolution trend requires a prior decision on starting point. I have chosen 1980 for that purpose, but other times would produce similar patterns.

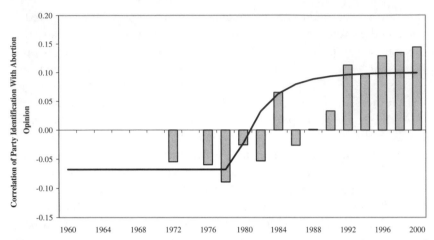

FIGURE 3.3. Correlations between partisanship and abortion attitudes: National Election Studies, 1960 to 2000. *Note:* See Figure 3.1.

can expect a more complete sorting by party over the coming few election cycles. As it becomes ever more the case that voters think about their abortion views when they choose to become Democrats or Republicans, what we do not expect is a reversal. The momentum of alignment pushes forward.

Thus all three cases we have seen are moving toward a settled conclusion. The fact that all three seem to be nearly over is a consequence of having chosen issues that have been around long enough to assess their history. Newer conflicts, such as that over gay rights, might well be in a take-off stage as these others conclude. But we can't know; the data are still too thin, the process too new.

Now, theory of new issues in hand, I am ready to proceed to the central questions: What do Americans want government to do, and how do preferences change over time?

PREFERENCES FOR LIBERALISM AND CONSERVATISM

We have seen in the last chapter that the New Deal welfare state issue cluster behaves as if most individual issues were virtually interchangeable. Imagine that we had taken the seven series of Figure 2.9 and just averaged them together. That single measure would tell us the net liberalism and conservatism of Americans, at least on this issue set. That is shown in Figure 3.4.

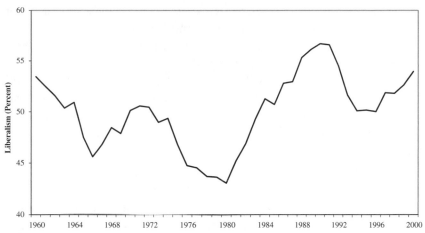

FIGURE 3.4. An estimate of national preference liberalism as an average of the seven welfare state issues of Figure 2.9.

The average naturally captures what was seen in all the individual series, liberalism in the early 1960s, followed by growing conservatism over the 1970s, peaking with the 1980 election of Ronald Reagan, followed by a return to liberalism in the run-up to Bill Clinton's 1992 recapture of the White House, followed by increased conservatism once Clinton took office. The simple average of Figure 3.4 is close to an answer to the question, "What do Americans want government to do?"

It isn't quite the whole answer because it excludes numerous small controversies that did not produce longtime series of survey questions, and of course it is only the welfare state/size of government dimension to American politics. More desirable would be a summary measure of all the dimensions of opinion that exist and one that incorporates everything in the record of surveyed domestic opinion. Also, the analysis thus far required me to make judgments about which items tapped which controversies, what belonged and what didn't. It would be desirable to have a measure that emerges free of such prior decisions.

For that we need a technology to accomplish the same feat as the averaging of Figure 3.4, but where averaging itself won't work. What we want is the ability to uncover the latent dimensions of attitude that lie beneath expressed preferences. Such a technology exists but would require a substantial digression into mathematics to describe it, which I choose not to do here.[12] Taking all domestic policy preferences ever measured

---

[12] But see Stimson 1998, appendix 1, for a treatment of the technique.

in the period from 1952 to 2001, we solve for the dimensions of latent opinion, the "considerations" in Zaller and Feldman's (1992) terms.

To put together things that are different requires that we have at least a common scheme for indexing the result of a survey question. That common scheme takes all the possible answers of a question and groups them into three categories: liberal responses, conservative responses, and neutral or missing responses.[13] It discards the neutral and creates an index that can be described as followes:

$$\text{liberalism index} = 100\left[\frac{\text{liberal percent}}{(\text{liberal percent} + \text{conservative percent})}\right]$$

Thus, imagine a question that asks whether or not government should do more in a particular area with responses of more, 30 percent; less, 20 percent; about the same (or other), 50 percent. Then the index is $100[30/(30+20)] = 60$. In this scheme, then, 50 is a neutral point that occurs when equal numbers prefer more and less government. The data for analysis consist of liberalism index scores for all the domestic policy preferences in the public record of survey research that are repeated in two or more years (so that change can be observed). These 2,144 individual survey findings are arranged into 181 series over time. The solution operates by explaining as much as possible of the variation over time in the 181 series with a small number of latent dimensions.

Figure 3.5 begins a description of the solution. Two latent dimensions are found. The first and considerably more powerful (explaining about 70% of the systematic variation), is the main left versus right dimension of American politics. A secondary dimension accounts for the remaining 30 percent.

We can get a sense of what the dimensions are by seeing which policy domains they are associated with. In Figure 3.5 I have selected for display the twenty-one series that are available for twenty or more years of the fifty-year span (1952 to 2001).[14] Each is a survey item (measured

---

[13] The direction of coding is arbitrary. It doesn't matter whether or not my judgment is right. If I got a particular item backward, it would work just as well and produce the same ultimate solution.

[14] The limitation on items to twenty or more years is from the numbers that can be displayed without confusion and overprinting. If the set were expanded beyond these, the next items, by order of loading on the first dimension, would be (1) education, (2) health, (3) race, (4) guns, (5) environment, (6) economics, (7) health, (8) race, (9) environment, (10) environment, (11) size of government, (12) size of government, and (13) health. The set of items in the figure is quite representative of those not displayed. Additions to the second dimension, however, are less clearly related to those displayed, leaving

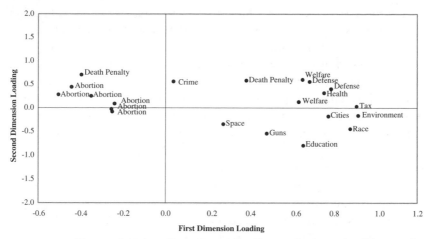

FIGURE 3.5. Two underlying dimensions of policy preferences: loadings on derived latent dimensions of preference. *Note:* Loadings are correlations between
individual item time series and the derived underlying dimensions of mood. Thus
both axes have a possible range of -1.0 to $+1.0$. The vertical axis is compressed
to represent its smaller explanatory power.

at multiple points in time), named here only by the domain from which
it comes. The items are displayed in space according to their loadings
(correlations with the underlying scale). The size of the loadings indicates
strength of association, that is, shared content, while the sign indicates
whether the items move with (positive) or against (negative) the underlying dimension.

The right-hand side of the figure, that is, those items that load strongly
on the main dimension, is the set of controversies that regularly divide
the two political parties: taxes, welfare, cities, environment, race, education, and so forth. Defense spending occupies much the same space.
Coded as the opposite of domestic spending preferences, it behaves as
the guns versus butter off-and-on debate would suggest. Those who want
more domestic spending want less defense spending, and vice versa. (If
defense had been coded the same as domestic issues, it would occupy the
extreme left-hand side of the figure. How it is coded does not matter for
the mathematics of the solution.)

The conflict over gun control, which does not have its roots in the New
Deal Party system, nonetheless behaves pretty much as if it were a standard

me cautious about the interpretation. The scale of the figure represents a 70-30 ratio of
importance of the two dimensions, showing more separation along the major horizontal
axis than along the minor vertical one.

part of the left-right cleavage. An issue on spending for space exploration shows a weaker alignment, which is consistent with its generally lesser salience in American politics.

The second dimension, up and down in the figure, is harder to interpret. Most notable is that the items that are highly positive have to do with crime and criminals. One is about how harshly convicted criminals should be treated and the other two concern the ultimate harsh penalty, death. At the other end, down in the figure, are issue preferences such as gun control and education, which might be considered alternate remedies for social deviance. Thus the dimension might be thought of as hard-line versus soft-line. Because the underlying dimension is weaker, as are most of the loadings on it, interpretation must be a little uncertain. One possibility is that this is merely the "plus" of the one-plus dimensions my little theory leads me to expect. If so, it may be no more than some systematic variation that clumps together as a kind of mathematical residue, but making no sense for politics.

Abortion, an issue on which there are numerous and excellent measures, does not particularly fit either dimension. But the cluster of abortion items in the same space on the left side clearly indicates that various abortion attitudes fit with one another, if with nothing else.[15] Indeed, the only reason the issue is included here is to demonstrate that it doesn't fit (and to avoid the appearance of choosing issues to get a desired result). The evidence says that it adds nothing to a measure of liberal or conservative preferences.

The purpose of dimensional analysis is not the analysis but extracting the dimensions that we uncover. That result is seen in Figure 3.6, where the two extracted dimensions are displayed. This, particularly the critical first dimension, is the result for which we have traveled a road of theory and number crunching in this chapter. It is the central measure of what Americans want from government.

So familiar that it hardly needs to be introduced, this extracted dimension, called Public Policy Mood in my earlier work (Stimson 1998; Erikson et al. 2002), looks just like the measure of preferences in Figure 3.4. The difference is that the former was based on a selected set of data and designed to appeal to reader intuition that the garden-variety average is a sensible way to combine several measures. This measure is the result of

---

[15] This lack of correlation results from using the full history of abortion preferences. Consistent with the issue evolution theory, if we used just the last few years we would see growing correlation with the left versus right issues.

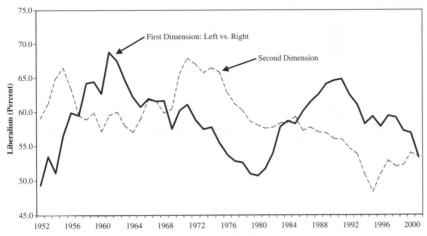

FIGURE 3.6. The derived two dimensions of policy preferences.

applying a dimensional analysis to all available survey items, even those, such as abortion preferences, known to follow a different track.

To put the matter bluntly, the first dimension of American public opinion is the welfare state/size of government controversy that divides the parties. That is definitely not a surprise. It is what we would have expected from a theory of issue spaces.

What do we make of Figure 3.6? Are the ups and downs of these measured preferences just zigs and zags, random movements around a stable level? Or do they follow a pattern? Are they meaningless or meaningful? One pattern emerges fairly strongly. Preferences "zig" upward (toward liberalism) when Republicans control the White House and "zag" downward when Democrats are in charge. Indeed, much of the observed movement of the figure is exactly that: movements in policy preference away from the chosen direction of the party in power.

These movements, it is important to note, are entirely in abstract preferences, where the questions make no references to the administration, its policies, or successes or failures therein. They ask respondents what they want "government" (or sometimes "the government in Washington" or "the federal government") to do. After a particular party is in power, and regardless of its standing, the public wants less of the kind of policies it is pursuing.

Figure 3.7 captures this effect. By merely taking the annual estimates and rearranging them as the beginning and end points of party spans of control of the presidency, that pattern emerges. The only periods in

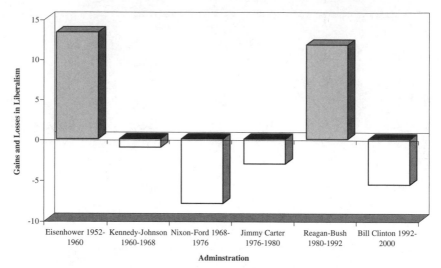

FIGURE 3.7. Liberal and conservative preference change by administration in power. *Note:* Bars represent the changes in mood between the beginning and end of a period of party control of the White House. The gray (positive) bars represent gains in liberalism. The white (negative) bars represent gains in conservatism.

which liberalism of preferences has gained ground have been during the Republican administrations of Eisenhower, Reagan, and the first George Bush. Three spans of Democratic control have produced most of the gains for conservatism in this half-century. The one exception, when preferences did not move contrary to the direction of the White House, was the 1968–76 period, when Richard Nixon and Gerald Ford left the nation more conservative than it was when Nixon took office.[16] Even including the exception, the three spans of Republican control produced a net gain of seventeen points in liberalism. The three spans of Democratic control similarly move the nation rightward by about ten points.

Does it matter? Look at elections as a test. Each of these spans of party control ended by a defeat at the hands of the opposition, and in each case preferences had moved beyond the tipping point in the direction of that successful opposition. This is seen most clearly in two Republican eras, the eight Eisenhower years and the twelve of Reagan and Bush. Both eras

---

[16] Perhaps we should point to Kennedy and Johnson as the exceptions. Because conservatism gained only a near trivial one point in the manifestly liberal 1960s, Richard Nixon inherited a very liberal public opinion – near its all-time high – and could not have been expected to move it further in that direction.

saw landslide reelections of popular Republican presidents followed by a quick turn to the other party.

We also bring expectations from our popular culture. It holds the 1960s to have been a time of great liberalism, the 1980s equally conservative, and so on. That also can be seen in Figure 3.6. Our single measure of preferences makes two full cycles, conservative to liberal to conservative to liberal and back again toward conservative. And two of these loops correspond to what our culture says should be the case. But there is a difference, too. The preference measure is ahead of cultural expectations. It shows the famous liberalism of the 1960s building in the late 1950s and peaking at the beginning of the decade, not at its middle or end. And the same story holds for the 1980s: The conservatism starts earlier and ends earlier than we might have thought. It is as if we notice the change in the cultural reflection of political views, not in the views themselves.

The liberalism we see of the 1960s is the liberalism that produced the Kennedy administration and then fueled it in full force at the outset of the civil rights movement. It is not the liberalism of the youth revolt or the anti–Vietnam War protest. These came later, after the political impetus of liberalism was spent. But it is the cultural manifestations that have come to color our images of the 1960s. They clearly were something different, a mass movement of style (its emphasis on lack thereof) more than substance. Long hair and ragged clothes produced no policy consequences to speak of. The impetus of liberalism had its last fling in the Great Society legislation of 1965. As the decade become the colorful time we remember, the U.S. government became as quiescent as it had been in the early Eisenhower era. There was much talk of politics in the era, not much action.

The 1980s are the mirror image of the 1960s. Conservatism peaked with the election of Ronald Reagan; it was not produced by him. The 1980s did see pretty fundamental change in Washington, but even more than the 1960s we can date it precisely. The first 100 days or so of the Reagan administration produced it all. The spring of 1981 saw Reagan's tax cut, his one serious effort to limit domestic spending, and the buildup of defense. The rest of the Reagan years, and the 1980s generally, were a time of conservative retreat. Just as we see in measured preferences, the nation saw then a public opinion that encouraged conservative action before it happened and then said "enough" when it did. Reagan was in command of the budget battle of 1981, the key time in which priorities were reshaped rightward. Seven subsequent Reagan budgets were labeled "dead on arrival" when sent up to the Hill.

The run-up to liberalism preceding Bill Clinton is less expected. Just as we were half a decade or so behind the curve expecting liberalism when we got Richard Nixon, the expectation of conservatism in the 1980s would not have predicted the electoral success of a Democrat.[17] But it appears as dramatic as the conservatism that produced Reagan twelve years before. And like that conservative trend, it began to disappear quickly after the election.

As we see the ebb and flow of preferences, beyond that picture we can also see the normal dominance of liberalism. All this ebb and flow takes place, that is, in the liberal end of the spectrum, above the neutral point of 50 on the graph. When Americans are asked whether they want government to do more or spend more – implicitly to tax more – in general they say "yes" a lot more often than "no." That conclusion springs from the hundreds of different sorts of survey questions that we have. The pattern is not universal. Americans do not want government to spend more on "welfare," for example. But over all issues and controversies, "more" dominates "less." Americans are operationally liberal; given a choice of more government or less, they generally choose more.

Does that mean that we are in some fundamental sense liberal? Not so fast. There is another angle to consider.

IDEOLOGY: OPERATIONAL AND SYMBOLIC

For a long time we have had a simpler approach to the matter of ideology: just asking. Since the mid-1950s survey organizations have posed a number of questions along the line of "Generally speaking, do you think of yourself as a conservative, a liberal, a moderate, or what?" And despite some misgivings about the quality of the measure, we have used the answers to characterize the American electorate.

Consider these self-descriptions the symbolic side of ideology. Respondents, in answering these sorts of questions, are associating themselves with the symbols of whatever it is that "liberal" and "conservative" mean. There is a problem with this symbolic ideology at the outset; about a third of those asked the question do not answer. They tell us that they don't

---

[17] This measure dates from an original produced in my 1991 book, which was subject to some public ridicule at the time, showing, as does the figure, that the current era was far from the conservatism that commentators all agreed was then dominant. Thus it is not that I have great political intuition; I was simply reporting what the data said (and more than I was prepared to believe). Perhaps the moral should be to treat political commentary with due skepticism.

think in those terms, that they don't know what the words mean, and they are right.[18] So we are characterizing only two-thirds of the American public, generally those who are better educated and more involved in politics, when we use these data.

So what do we learn simply by asking? The picture is quite different from what we have seen from policy preferences. The most striking difference is that on average, the answer is opposite. While we have seen that most Americans prefer a government that does more rather than less – they are, that is, operationally liberal – when asked to describe political identity, almost two of three choose the label "conservative" over the label "liberal." The joint conclusion, something we have long observed (Free and Cantril 1967), is that Americans on average are symbolically conservative and operationally liberal. This is a puzzle that needs a solution, a problem that will gain my focus for the remainder of this chapter.

Before observing the trends in symbolic ideology, it is worth noting how much confusion this puzzle causes our politics. Because both sides of the puzzle are reliably true, commentators on both side of American politics can always make their case about the "real" America, even while disagreeing fiercely with one another. Look at symbolic ideology, and it is true that conservatism dominates liberalism. Look at preferences for what government does, and it is true that preferences most of the time favor more rather than less. It is tempting in this puzzling situation to resolve it by asking which of these findings is real and which is illusion. But that won't get us far because both sides seem quite real. The contradiction is in the views of the American people, not just in the analysis.

The basic facts of ideological self-identification are captured in Figure 3.8, a compilation of nineteen different series of queries, 1,162 individual readings in all. The most striking fact of the responses is the dominance of conservative over liberal identifications. Setting aside the large numbers of people who don't use the words at all or call themselves "moderates"[19] – together almost half of all those asked the question – on average about 62 percent of the remaining half who take sides take the

---

[18] On occasion prompts are added to force a response even after respondents have said that they do not think in ideological terms, usually on the order of "Well, if you were forced to choose one of those two, which one would it be?" What we learn from doing so is that the responses to the follow-up seem quite meaningless, telling us that respondents weren't being reticent about their views; they truly didn't know what the words meant.

[19] I have little to say of symbolic moderates because we can't separate true moderates – those who know what the debate is about and choose a middle position – from the numerous respondents who don't know what the words connote at all and therefore grab onto "moderate" as a safe response that does not require them to admit their ignorance.

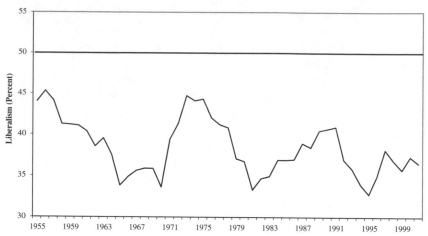

FIGURE 3.8. Ideological self-identification: percent liberal of those who classify themselves "liberal" or "conservative."

conservative side. The variation around that is quite small, with liberalism commanding the identification of 45 percent of Americans at its peak and reaching a low of 33 percent on several occasions.

Notice also what we do not see. One might expect to see liberalism in the 1960s, conservatism in the 1980s, and so on, our cultural memory of the eras of American politics. What the data say, in contrast, is that conservatism has always been the dominant symbolic preference of American voters. The variation in it is not "then" and "now"; the observed cycles are of shorter duration. They appear large in the figure only because the range of variation is so small than any movement looks large. On a scale of the possible range of 0 to 100, the series would look like a flat line with an occasional small movement. These small movements, however, are highly systematic. With huge numbers of individual surveys contributing to the estimates, the bumps and wiggles are definitely not chance variation.

I have put off the question of what people mean when they style themselves "liberal" or "conservative." We know what politicians and commentators mean when they use those words, usually the size and scope of government.[20] Do ordinary people mean the same thing, and do they

[20] Political theorists write a lot about "liberalism" with a wholly different connotation. Indeed, the nineteenth-century liberalism concepts virtually define what is commonly meant by conservatism. I use the "street" connotation, the one that aligns with the party system.

mean it consistently? The answer to both questions appears to be "no." As we see below, some don't know what the words mean at all. Others use the words in a fashion that changes with the times. That helps to explain some of the movements in Figure 3.8. The high point of modern liberalism, for example, is seen in the early 1970s, when "liberal" briefly meant that someone was opposed to the Vietnam War. Further, we know that what liberals and conservatives in the public think the words mean differs. That is, they do not see themselves at opposite ends of the same issue debate, but see the issues differently (Conover and Feldman 1981). It is like a tug-of-war between two sides that can't agree what is the rope they are pulling on.

To deal with these questions of connotation and to untangle the puzzle of symbolic conservatism and operational liberalism, we need to turn to individual responses. That is my task here.

Why Is It That So Many "Conservatives" Want Bigger Government?

The National Opinion Research Center's General Social Surveys offer an opportunity to deal with individual response and change over time. Incorporating twenty-two separate cross-sectional surveys from 1973 through 2000, they allow us to look at individual attitudes and connect them to one another. In particular, we can isolate "symbolic" liberalism and conservatism and then associate that with the operational attitudes that appear to be in conflict.

The easy part is isolating the symbolic ideologues. A common question on self identification allows that:

We hear a lot of talk these days about liberals and conservatives. I'm going to show you a seven-point scale on which the political views that people might hold are arranged from extremely liberal – point 1 – to extremely conservative – point 7. Where would you place yourself on this scale?

In this way, we can let liberals and conservatives be who they say they are. Then we can build scales of attitude to approximate the preferences isolated in Figure 3.6. For that task I chose six items on spending for national priorities, focusing on those that come from the New Deal issue cluster and divide the parties.[21] Each of them asks whether spending is

---

[21] Others, not used, ask about such things as highways, space travel, and national parks and do not divide the population along the same lines as do the traditional fights over big government.

too little, too much, or about right for the issue in question. The issues chosen are education, race, cities, environment, health care, and welfare, the traditional battleground of the welfare state.

For each issue we know how liberal and conservative politicians stand: Liberals consistently advocate more in each area and conservatives less. Those who respond that spending is "too little" we regard as operational liberals and score $+1$. Those who say it is "too much" we regard as operational conservatives and score -1. The neutral "about right" we score as 0. Then for the six program areas, adding up the scores gives us a net operational liberalism measure with a possible range of -6 to $+6$. We know from earlier analyses to expect that the electorate will be more liberal on average – it has to be if there are more conservatives than liberals but people prefer more to less spending on average.

The spending data, summarized over the 36,000 people interviewed over the span of 1973 to 2000, are given in Figure 3.9. This figure shows the operational liberalism we expect. That is, the net preference of the whole electorate is for increased spending. The median preference of $+2$ is consistent with preferences to increase four programs and cut two, to increase two and cut none, and so forth. Increases on average dominate cuts. This electorate is operationally "liberal" by definition. If we looked at only those who called themselves conservatives, the pattern is

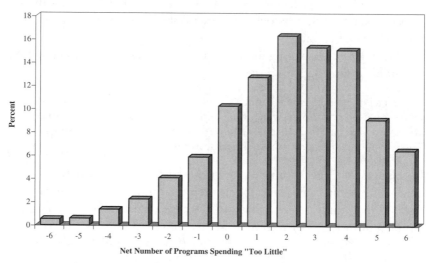

FIGURE 3.9. Domestic spending preferences of self-described conservatives: net percent saying "too little" in six program areas. *Note:* Bars represent "net" spending preferences: number of domestic programs to increase minus number to decrease.

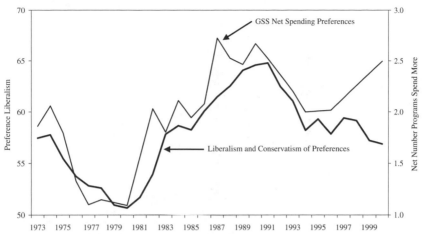

FIGURE 3.10. General Social Survey net spending preferences compared with preference liberalism from Figure 3.6, 1972 to 2000.

strikingly similar. Conservatives are on average less liberal, with a mean of +1.28 as opposed to the +2.04 of all respondents, but not very much. The self-styled conservatives, wanting to increase more domestic spending programs than they cut, are, on average, liberal!

The issue is how symbolic and operational attitudes align or fail to. Are symbolic liberals (by self-identification) operational liberals (by preference)? Are symbolic conservatives also operational conservatives? Before we address that central concern, we need to satisfy ourselves that the preferences measured at the individual level in the GSS studies are related to the preferences extracted from the survey research record. When we recover the time dimension in these data, does it track what we already know? That is accomplished in Figure 3.10, where exactly the same preference series from the earlier Figure 3.6, the first dimension of policy preferences, is displayed against the average for all GSS respondents by year on spending for the six welfare state programs. The measurement scales are different. Preferences (on the left vertical axis) are measured as the net percentage choosing the liberal side. The GSS net spending indicator (on the right vertical axis) is scored as the average number of programs to be increased over those to be cut.

Clearly, these two measures of the same preference for big government track one another well over time. They are about as highly correlated as is possible for two independently estimated series. That means that the spending data, on average, form a valid indicator of operational ideology.

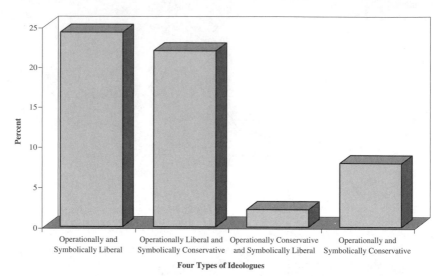

FIGURE 3.11. The composition of self-declared ideologues (moderates excluded) by consistency with domestic spending preferences.

The goal of this individual-level measurement exercise is that with both operational and symbolic measures for each respondent, we can now confront the contradiction between symbolic and operational. The zero neutral point on the spending scale is a natural cut point. We call those who want to increase more than cut "operational liberals," and those who want to cut more than increase "operational conservatives." Excluding the confusing symbolic moderates and those at the zero neutral point on spending, we are left with four possibilities. Two of them are the obvious cases, consistent liberals and conservatives who combine symbolic and operational ideologies, "conservatives" who want to cut government spending, "liberals" who want to increase it. More interesting are the inconsistent cases, particularly the numerous symbolic conservatives who are operational liberals.

Figure 3.11 shows that the symbolically conservative and operational liberal are a very large group, 22 percent of all GSS respondents over the years. These tens of millions of people, to be called "conflicted conservatives,"[22] are the beginning of the resolution of the operational-symbolic puzzle. Lots of people think of themselves as conservatives and act as

---

[22] There are many ways to name this category of the public, since they present a mix of both liberal and conservative. "Conservative" with the adjective "conflicted" honors their own preference in the matter. They call themselves "conservatives."

liberals. The opposite group, operational conservatives who are symbolic liberals, at only 2 percent of the electorate, is easier to understand; they probably just do not know what "liberal" and "conservative" are supposed to mean. Something more systematic must explain the conflicted conservatives.

Who Are the Conflicted Conservatives?

Given the high level of observed inconsistency between operation and symbol, there are two routes to an explanation. We can ask why the conservative symbol is so popular, or why the liberal spending is. Each presumes that the inconsistency can be resolved.

Imagine somebody who has newly arrived in America, let's say from Mars, where there may or may not be life, but there are no liberals or conservatives. Confronted with the knowledge that one side is called liberal (but does not call itself that) and the other side conservative, how might our Martian choose? Well, having learned the English language to communicate with Earthlings, he or she might gravitate toward "conservative." Knowing nothing about politics, the word "conservative" often connotes "thoughtful," "hardheaded," and "prudent." We approve conservative estimates, conservative hypotheses, and conservative investments. Stripped of political content, "conservative" is a good thing, an adjective more likely to praise than condemn. "Liberal" is not so good. Liberal sex is promiscuity. Liberal graders lack standards. In general, outside politics the word is closely synonymous with "easy," meaning overboard and without discipline. So perhaps some number of those who style themselves "conservative" just like the image and really do not know the political content of the word.

The alternative tack is to treat the symbolic attachment as real and meaningful and then question whether attitudes toward spending are really operationally liberal. It is possible that citizens can approve of more spending in a variety of areas and not consider that somebody – and ultimately probably they themselves – will have to pay for it. There is some evidence that this is true; enthusiasm for spending always outdistances willingness to increase taxes.[23] But we shall see below that symbolic

---

[23] But beware the facile conclusion that people just aren't smart enough to grasp the connection between spending and taxing. We know what citizens hear about government spending, both from politicians and independently from the mass media. That message is perfectly uniform: that much government spending is wasteful and unnecessary. Thus it is

conservatives do not look very conservative on other sorts of issues thought to divide liberals and conservatives.

We can learn a little by isolating the conflicted conservatives and asking what kinds of people they are. We know that gender is associated with political views, that women more likely to be liberal, and men conservative. This is more strikingly so among consistent liberals and conservatives, with women 54 percent liberal and men only 38. The gender break among the conflicted conservatives, 53 to 47, looks like that of liberals. We would expect an association with education, since being conflicted implies not knowing well what the political terms mean. There is an association, but not as strong as I would have expected. About 66 percent of consistent liberals and conservatives have high school education or less. This rate rises to 74 percent among conflicted conservatives. Voter turnout, which often is associated with attributes of political sophistication, is only slightly associated with being conflicted between operational and symbolic ideology. Consistent conservatives vote at a very high level in presidential elections, 84 percent by self-report for the most recent presidential election. Consistent liberals are less likely to vote, reporting 68 percent turnout. The conflicted conservatives look like the liberals on turnout, with a rate of 69 percent.

Are the operationally liberal symbolic conservatives really liberal? On a frequently posed question that gets at the divide over the fundamental role of government in reducing the income differences that emerge from the private economy, the conservative position is that government should stay out of it. Yet 36 percent of all self-identified conservatives advocate government efforts to equalize incomes, and that rises to 43 percent among the conflicted operationally liberal conservatives as opposed to the mere 19 percent among the consistent conservatives.

On a wholly different and wholly noneconomic issue, capital punishment, the conservative position is support. That is seen in a 90–10 ratio of support over opposition among consistent conservatives. Opposition rises to a still minority 21 percent opposition among the conflicted conservatives. And 77 percent of conflicted conservatives advocate required gun permits. On affirmative action, the conflicted conservatives are almost exactly in between consistent liberals and consistent conservatives. On government involvement to guarantee jobs, they split 28 to 28 for and

not inconsistent for citizens to believe that much more could be spent on their approved priority programs and that the new spending could come from that giant reservoir that Ronald Reagan called "waste, fraud, and abuse." President Reagan, it should be noted, never could find those lines in the budget that candidate Reagan marked for elimination.

against, the rest neutral. On government involvement in general, 28 percent call for more, as against 36 percent wanting less. These people are not very conservative.

Nor are the conflicted conservatives social conservatives or closet racists. Nor are they falsely conscious of their social position. They see themselves much like consistent liberals and conservatives. In these areas, too, they are in between real liberals and real conservatives, not really one or the other. If we are going to call them "conservatives" – what they call themselves – then we have to reformulate our idea of conservatism to make it look a lot like liberalism.

Does it matter at all that these people who seem pretty liberal in their preferences think of themselves as conservatives? Yes, it does. It means that candidates and parties that call themselves by that same label will in general be more appealing to them. Because they think of themselves as conservative, Republican candidates are much more appealing to them than their liberal preferences would dictate. Consistent liberals report having voted for the Democratic candidate in the most recent presidential election, (relative to the year in which they were interviewed), 77 percent of the time, compared with 15 percent for the consistent conservatives. The conflicted conservatives are in between, at 38 percent, pulled both ways by liberal preferences and conservative symbols. And it is the same story for party identification. The conflicted conservatives are a little more Republican (37%) than Democratic (32%), but not decisively on one side or the other, as are consistent liberals and conservatives.

This gives some leverage on electoral politics in America. Divide all voters into four groups, the consistent liberals and conservatives, on the one hand, and the conflicted conservatives and wholly nonideological "moderates," on the other. The consistent ideologues are written off by both parties as beyond reach. They are the core ideological constituencies of the two parties. Elections then center on the battleground groups, the nonideological and the conflicted conservatives. The nonideological do not respond to ideological appeals, and so the parties seek their votes by claiming that they are more competent, more patriotic, and more moral than the opposition. The parties promise results to them of peace and prosperity, not policies.

The conflicted conservatives are the interesting group. Large enough to swing all elections one way or the other, their votes are potentially available to both parties. They want liberal policies and respond to specific Democratic appeals to do more and spend more on various domestic priorities. They think of themselves as conservatives and respond to

Republican identification with conservatism. Which has the stronger appeal, liberal policies or conservative symbols, is a close call and so varies with the times. Where demand for liberal policies is at a low ebb as in 1980, symbols prevail and Republicans win. When that demand is strong – think 1960 or 1992 – then the policies carry the day and Democrats win. That makes these voters hugely important in determining outcomes.

The conflicted conservatives dictate normal campaign strategy for both parties. From the Democratic side the liberal policies are an asset and the liberal symbol is a liability. The strategy for dealing with this is to emphasize the specific, over and over, saying, "We will do this, we will do that, we will do the other thing," all the while staying as far away from the symbol "liberal" as is possible. Democratic candidates never call themselves liberals; they know it is bad politics. (We "know" that they are liberals, but that knowledge comes from their Republican opponents, who brand them "liberal" at every opportunity.) Bill Clinton is the archetype of the successful Democratic appeal. Calling himself a "new Democrat," the meaning of which is exactly "not liberal," his every speech was rich in detailed policy proposals. Called a "policy wonk," for every problem in America he had thought about what sorts of government action would be useful and was willing to propose it. Clinton's whole eight-year administration can be seen as a struggle between policy and symbols. When Clinton could deal in policy specifics, as, for example, in his State of the Union speeches, his public standing was high; Americans were willing to follow where he led. When he was successfully tarred by "liberal" symbolism, as for example, in the 1994 midterm election after two years of liberal symbolism, he could find no audience for his policy proposals.

The Republican strategic imperative is opposite. Republicans do well when they deal in symbols and lose ground when they talk specific policies; symbols are an asset, policies a liability. So Republican candidates call themselves "conservative" at every opportunity; they craft speeches to allow them say it in many different ways and not appear repetitive. And of course one way of saying it is to call their opponents "liberals," which they also do as often as opportunity permits. The Republican tack on policies is to talk ends over means, general dispositions over specific plans. Matched head to head, Republican policy proposals will usually lose the competition to Democratic proposals. Republicans cannot credibly claim to do more or spend more than the party that is known for doing and spending. So not allowing that head-to-head confrontation is the smart thing for Republicans to do. Democrats say, "I will do *x*." Republicans say, "I have a plan to achieve x" and do not talk about its details. They would avoid policy proposals altogether if they could, but it would be a disadvantage for one party to appear to have a plan and the other not. So talking about goals and talking about plans without specifying details is what works. George W. Bush illustrates to Republican strategy well. Calling himself a "compassionate conservative," the practical meaning of which was a conservative who would spend money on education, he at once combined the symbolic appeal of conservatism and neutralized a Democratic advantage on education spending. His every speech and debate emphasized his general conservative orientation toward government. His opponent, Gore, said what he would do. Faced with the same questions, Bush said what attitude he would bring (pragmatic conservatism) toward dealing with the same issues.

Long-term flows of opinion this way and that are the backdrop of American politics. They do not dictate its outcomes, but they do determine what is possible, which appeals will work at one time and not another. In the next chapter I take this all as given and focus again on ebb and flow, but on the day-to-day, looking at how the public responds to political campaigns as they happen: in the horse race.

4

The Great Horse Race

Finding Meaning in Presidential Campaigns

Democrats were in the dumps. In the beginning of election year 2000 they had an unusually good record to run on, but a candidate they believed was a stiff. From the time of Bill Clinton's reelection in 1996, it was evident that Al Gore would seek election to the presidency in 2000 – and it was evident to most that he would lose. As election season dawned, some party leaders kept a stiff upper lip about Gore's prospects. But those who were free to speak their minds were uniform in assessing his chances as poor and in blaming the poor chances on Al Gore himself.

Gore was wooden and uncomfortable, and his proper blue suit demeanor screamed "politician" to a nation leery of politicians. The public knew little of Gore and what it knew was mainly bad news. Gore had done something unsavory, maybe illegal, in a Buddhist temple. He had done fund raising in 1996 from the White House. But more than that, he just didn't seem to have "it." Standing beside Bill Clinton was an always unfavorable comparison for Gore. One of the most remarkable politicians of all times, Clinton's chemistry with voters seemed so nearly magical that nothing he did in office – where he set new standards for presidential embarrassment in the Lewinsky episode – seemed to matter. Gore, whose behavior was exemplary in contrast, evoked no warmth or trust.

Republicans at the same time expressed a confidence not seen since Ronald Reagan's 1984 landslide. George W. Bush raised massive sums of money the year before the campaign and consolidated the support of the Republican establishment before the primary season began. His outmaneuvered and ill-funded opponents tested him only briefly before conceding in early March that Bush had already won the Republican nomination. Bush's lead over Gore in the early season horse race polls was so substantial that most Republicans were openly assuming that the White House was theirs, planning already early in the year 2000 for the January 2001 transition to power. After a well-scripted show of unity (which was real) and diversity (which was not real) in the Republican convention in late July, the already substantial lead ballooned from the convention bounce to a level that appeared insurmountable. It looked then as if Gore's best chance was to put on an equally successful show – which is what American presidential nominating conventions have become – at which point he might get back to trailing Bush by only seven or eight points by Labor Day. But a seven- or eight-point lead on Labor Day is a pretty sure thing.

But something happened. Out in the country people started to like Gore. He got the customary bounce from a Democratic convention, which all agreed was not as good a show as the Republican gathering two weeks earlier. And then, when the afterglow was gone and the bounce should have ended, it did not. Gore, the underdog, actually moved into a tie and then a small lead. Commentators, prepared to explain Gore's unpopularity and defeat, were hard-pressed to account for his growing popularity. Maybe it was the big kiss he planted on his wife Tipper, they said. But the evidence was otherwise, and less dramatic. Even while he was trailing badly in the horse race polls, Al Gore's image was growing more positive. That trend was well under way before the humanizing and much-discussed kiss.

Here is a less dramatic story. Vice presidents, *all* vice presidents, have an image problem. Part of this is the long tradition in the press of treating the vice president with derision. It seems a normal aspect of American life that these people, highly impressive outside the context of the peculiar office they hold, are expected to be fools, lightweights, and grist for stand-up comedy.

But we don't need to rely on such a loose cultural explanation. There is a peculiar aspect of the vice presidency that predicts that "veeps" should often have image problems. Vice presidents, like their running mates, take a lot of public criticism. And that is particularly the case in situations such as Gore's, where the vice president is expected to be the nominee in the next election. Unlike presidents, however, vice presidents have virtually no ability to answer the criticism. The president has the "bully pulpit" from which he or she can fire back at opponents. It is an even contest. Vice presidents take the incoming fire and do not fire back; absorbing abuse is virtually part of the job description.

What we should expect, then, is that after a lengthy period in office all vice presidents will have an image that is systematically unfavorable, relative to their true talents and qualities of person. That leads us to expect that vice presidents will perform poorly early in their campaigns for the top job, bearing the burden of the accumulated poor image. But images are capable of changing, particularly if they are based on relatively little knowledge or exposure on the part of the public. When will they change? Precisely when the unaware public "meets" the vice president on his or her own terms. That can occur at many moments along the campaign, but the most likely one, where the vice president gets huge and wholly positive exposure, is the party convention.

So the story of Gore's gains in mid-2000 is that the public saw Gore on his own terms for the first time, and some small portion of it (probably people most inclined to support a Democratic candidate in the first place) revised its view from buffoon who did something in a Buddhist temple to the real Al Gore, an attractive figure.

I could have changed the dates to 1988 and written the same story about the strange emergence of the elder George Bush from "wimp" standing. Like Gore twelve years later, Bush began his race looking like a small figure in the shadow of Ronald Reagan. It was hard to take seriously a guy who was considered a little goofy.[1] But when image doesn't fit reality, reality – if a candidate has an opportunity to show it – will change image. The story of 1988 most often told is the famous "Willie Horton" ad, where Bush played the race card to discredit Michael Dukakis.[2] Such events are always emphasized well out of proportion to their true impact. I would not go so far as to say that it meant nothing. But if I really want to understand why George Bush won a come-from-behind victory, I would point to his ability to show himself not to be the pathetic figure of his

---

[1] The Reagan-Bush comparison illustrates how hard the vice presidency can be on a candidate image. Reagan had a public standing much enhanced by the heroic sports and combat hero figures he had played in the movies. Bush, who suffered badly by comparison to Reagan, *was* a genuine war hero and *was* an accomplished athlete. While Reagan made war movies George Bush flew combat missions from an aircraft carrier in the brutal Pacific war. Bush nonetheless was called a "wimp" by the press.

[2] The race card interpretation comes most often from liberals and Democrats. An interpretation more sympathetic to the Bush campaign would note that much of Dukakis's early popularity was based on a false public perception that the former Massachusetts governor had quite moderate political views. An opponent almost necessarily would be required to shake that misperception in contrast to real Dukakis positions. The Willie Horton ad was part of a larger Bush strategy to shake that moderate image in contrast to Dukakis's record.

vice presidential image as the key factor moving votes. It doesn't make as dramatic a story. But I think it has the virtue of being true.

If this were a script for a TV drama, we'd have Gore go on to win. And he did, of course, win the popular vote. But he didn't win quite enough of it – by a few hundred contested ballots in Florida (and by a party-line vote in the Supreme Court) – and lost the contest that mattered. But the little Gore drama tells us something that matters, that the campaign for the presidency might affect who wins and who loses; all may not be preordained. The 2000 campaign may not be a particularly good case from which to learn this lesson, because its razor-thin outcome could have been switched by any number of otherwise trivial differences and oddities. In sports it would have been called a tie, settled by a "sudden death" scoring opportunity in overtime. But if we step back from the all-important question of who won and who lost, the impressive story-line of election 2000 is that Gore came from being so far back that he was written off to win a narrow popular vote victory (and a larger one than John F. Kennedy's 1960 showing).

The reader may be forgiven for thinking that I am asserting the obvious when I write that all may not be preordained. This is because most voters do not think it is. And the press, which is their information source, loves to write of presidential contests as horse races, the contestants surging forward or falling back with each day's new polls. But political science, as we see below, has developed a tendency toward belief that campaigns may be only a sideshow, where the main event is the state of the nation and, in particular, the nation's economy.[3]

THE LORE OF PRESIDENTIAL CAMPAIGNS: THREE STORIES

Presidential campaigns make good drama. Much, accordingly, is written of them; heavy library shelves contain tomes about all modern campaigns. They are full of events, observations, and interpretations. The style of my little story of the Gore 2000 campaign is not atypical of the genre. Authors try to be comprehensive, and so it would be inaccurate to say that they take only a single perspective. But the interpretations that emerge have emphases, which might be characterized as one of three common ones: the press story of the day-to-day campaign, the campaign professionals'

---

[3] I choose my words "tendency toward belief" carefully here, because it would be a mis-statement of the facts to claim a consensus on this view. But serious scholars advance the "sideshow" view, and they are taken seriously.

story of the campaign as a war among TV spots, and the political science story, which is quite different from either of the first two. The press story, what all of us are exposed to, will be most familiar.

The Press

Reporters travel with the candidates. That simple fact is important for understanding the press perspective on campaigns. To travel with the candidates is to be exposed to a daily grind of prearranged events in which candidates give speeches, shake hands, and kiss babies. Sometimes the candidates go through the motions, delivering the standard stump speech with professional effort, if not passion, to an audience that responds with politeness and curiosity about the strange business of politics. Sometimes the candidates connect with a receptive audience and it becomes a kind of romantic dance in which both partners loosen their normal inhibitions. This day-to-day campaign, of speeches, statements, gaffes, and occasional chemistry is what reporters see.

For months on end they travel, on and off airplanes, on and off buses. And they notice, too, that sometimes campaigns are fun and sometimes they are dreary. And sometimes travel arrangements are seamless and sometimes they are messed up. Sometimes candidates enliven press reporting by giving access to their inner thoughts. More often the reporters settle for what the public hears and get background only from people whose job is to feed the press a strategically calculated diet. This set of experiences, how it is to be on the road with the polls ever looming in the background as a reality check on impressions, is what reporters know and therefore what they write.

And so they write about the campaign as a sequence of daily events. The campaign is what happens on the road. And they notice that sometimes the campaigns seem to work, to touch people more than usually happens in politics. And sometimes candidates flail and fail to connect, trying first this and then that for the breakthrough that never comes. Reporters see this scene and report it, day after day, for months. The norm of their calling is that they should write about facts that they have witnessed and collected. And so they write about the campaign, how it is going on the road. When they see candidates connect with audiences and score points, they naturally conclude that they have witnessed a good campaign by a good candidate. And when they see candidates flail about and connect only with the party faithful, they naturally conclude that they have witnessed a bad campaign by a bad candidate. If they did anything very different, it would not be "reporting" as that term is understood and approved in professional journalism.

The point of this is that the decision to send reporters on the road with the candidates leads naturally to an interpretation of presidential elections mainly in terms of the skill and organization of the campaign on the road. That would be true if the campaign on the road were truly the campaign that mattered. And it would also be true if the other stories were correct, that the real campaign was the TV ad war, for which the events and speeches are just the backdrop. And it would also be true if the campaign didn't matter at all, if voters were just awaiting their November opportunity to do what had been determined by events and conditions long before the active campaign began.

Reporting on the road also leads to press interpretations of the outcome that are heavily flavored by the road campaign. Candidates win because they are good candidates running good campaigns. They lose because they are not good and preside over disorganized and strategically inept campaigns. This story is always told in the aftermath. There is a silliness to this ritual interpretation that Gelman and King (1993) point out. American politics is a very competitive business. Candidates who lack political skills have many opportunities to get weeded out – and they do. Winning a party nomination for the presidency is near the pinnacle of success for American politicians. It doesn't happen from luck. Candidates have to have something and they have to prove it many, many times before advancing to that stage. So how could it be that half of all major party candidates turn out to be inept, don't know how to campaign (after having won the nomination after a lifetime of successful campaigning)?

And the same story holds for the professionals who plan and operate the campaign. Presidential campaigns are money-is-no-object affairs in which both sides can and do recruit staffs that are deep in talent and experience. It just can't be the case that half of these organizations turn out to be incompetent, don't understand political strategy, don't know how to mount an effective campaign. And often both candidates and campaign staff who have just run an inept campaign (i.e., they lost) are the same people who have been praised for their political brilliance in past campaigns, where they won.

"Our candidate was a stiff who ran a bad campaign and made dumb mistakes" is an appealing story for the losing side. And no doubt press postmortems that emphasize the failure of talent and strategy draw heavily from insider commentary from the losing camp. The alternative, after all, is to say that the party's message was effectively articulated but rejected by the voters. The future is bright for the bad candidate, bad campaign story. You just do better next time. To concede that you did your best and still lost requires a searching reevaluation of what the party stood for and whether it should change.

Election Night Silliness: The Exit Poll

Much that is said about exit polling is nonsense. Exit polls – based on interviews with voters at polling places after they have voted – are a very good way of calling the winner in an election. Compared with polls that try to predict the winner in advance, they are like shooting ducks in a barrel. Voters are, after all, reporting what they have already done, not what they might do. And all of the problems of figuring out – which might more accurately be called guessing – which respondents will actually vote and which will not disappear. One hundred percent of those who emerge from the polls have voted.[4]

Professionals know how to do them correctly and they should be right nearly always (where "right" sometimes means "too close to call"). And they are. They so rarely fail that failure becomes newsworthy. What is notoriously unreliable is the alternative, actual vote counts. Until 100 percent of all precincts have reported vote counts, not only might the counts be seriously biased, but they often are. Central cities, suburbs, and outlying rural areas predictably divide their votes differently. And, predictably, they use different voting technologies that lead them to report at different times, some quickly, some only after long delay. Worse yet, since the technology of counting the vote is in constant flux, we don't do a very good job of anticipating just what those biases will be in the current campaign. And so in every election we know not to trust partial vote counts, but never quite know why. Real votes have a mystical standing in the civil religion of democracy. We just shouldn't confuse such reverence with the idea that they are a good information source on election night. They are not.

In the drama of election night, a drama that sells a lot of expensive advertising, exit polls come in mysteriously just when the polls close. In the typical scenario, the polls in a state close at 8:00 and the networks "call" the state at 8:01. The reality that most insiders know is that exit

---

4 Actually it should be said that all "think" that they have voted. One of the lessons of the Florida contest of 2000 is that the percentage of spoiled ballots is high enough to emerge as a serious threat to exit poll reports. This wasn't by any means new in 2000. It is just that the near tied result forced us to look seriously at the spoiled ballot issue.

poll results may be known quite early on election day. There is always the possibility that morning voters may have slightly different preferences than those who wait in lines as the polls close, but this doesn't have a history of mattering. So the exit poll for a state could be completed by noon of election day and the result could be called then. Voters – and no less losing candidates – take great offense at the idea of reporting the result when all of it hasn't yet happened.[5] And so the networks hold off until the polls close to tell us what they might have known for several hours. This is harmless, and I have to admit that I enjoy the drama of election night.

Silliness emerges when we *interpret* exit poll results. Excellent for factual reporting of how people have voted, exit polls have limited value for explaining *why*. They can be used to say *who* voted how, apportioning differences by fixed demographic attributes, such as black or white, male or female, urban or rural. It is the important *why* that doesn't work. It is customary to ask voters what issues were important to them and sometimes what positions they took on campaign issues. It is foolish to believe that what they say explains why they voted. What we observe, instead, are mainly post hoc rationalizations. Imagine being the voter being surveyed. You are asked how you have voted and what issues were important to you. From the perspective of the pollster, you are not being "tested," assessed to see whether your political savvy measures up. But from your own perspective, probably you see it as a test. So you have just reported voting for George W. Bush in 2000 and now you are asked something such as, "Which was more important to you, a major tax cut or adding a prescription drug benefit to Medicare?" Aha, it *is* a test. There is a correct answer, the tax cut, which candidate Bush has talked about at every opportunity for the past year. If your true preference was the Medicare enhancement, now you need to explain to yourself why you have just chosen the candidate who emphasized something else. People don't like inconsistency, and we would be foolish to expect them to express it.

And the interpretation that emerges on election night – "People who thought the tax cut was more important voted for Bush, 3 to 1" (or

---

[5] The 1980 Reagan victory is a well-studied case – see Jackson 1983 and Delli Carpini 1984 – of early calls and a rare early concession. Jackson finds that the early network calls of an impending landslide Reagan win, followed by Carter's early concession, did create lower turnout among those who had not yet voted. But those who intended to go the the polls and heard the news before voting made up a small proportion of the electorate, and the effect on their turnout was not large. In that case it was the winning party voters who were more affected.

something like that) – means nothing more than that 75 percent passed the test, correctly matching candidate to message. What it doesn't mean is that the tax cut proposal had absolutely anything to do with the outcome. I don't know whether it did or not. What I know is that if it did, the exit poll interpretation could not tell us that it did.

Advertising and Campaign Professionals

The professionals who run political campaigns see a different dynamic. Their whole definition of what the campaign is about is different. To them the campaign is about images, both of their own candidate and of the opponent. The point of a campaign is to decide what image a candidate should have and to build it, ad by ad. The professionals start the contest with a laundry list of strengths and liabilities. Their candidate is too young, too old, too inexperienced, too much a pol, soft or uncaring. Candidates who lack kids and dogs need to work on family image. Those who don't give a damn about their fellow citizens need to be seen as caring. The ad campaign is all about taking that starting image and then systematically assaulting the airwaves with messages that picture the candidate as he or she needs to be seen.

Professionals do polls, not so much to gauge momentum as to measure whether their ads are building the image they want. Image is loose and general. It is answers to questions such as "cares about people like me." And of course it matters who the "me" in question is. The ads go to great lengths to build images without words. Since the candidate is likely to be the star in most spots, what the image-builders can manage is who else is in the shot. You can learn a lot about strategy by watching spots and studying the background, not the foreground. Who are those admiring people the candidate is talking to? If candidate A is in trouble with the women's vote, they will be women. If weak on education, they'll be kids. Unlike issue claims, image spots make no promises that have to be kept and are unimpeded by the truth of past behavior. The candidate who hasn't been generous with education and doesn't intend to be if elected is the one who will do the "kids" image spot.

The advertising dynamic is punch and counterpunch. "We ran the 'cares about women' spot while they were doing 'tough on crime.' So we came back with our own crime spot which planted suggestions that his record was soft." To talk to the managers is to talk about image and how it is shaped by ads. The campaigns start off with independent strategies in the beginning, each a careful plan to build an image for election day. The dynamic of debate emerges later. The professionals watch the opposition's ads. When they think the opponents are scoring points, the careful plan is junked in favor of response. Just as the working press sees the stump speech as the "real" campaign, the managers focus on the one thing they control: which ads to run. They come to see the ad war as the essence of politics and the explanation for success and failure.

To talk to the managers on both sides of a political campaign, at least to me, is to be amazed by the degree to which they agree on what the fight was about and who scored the telling blows. Behind the scenes and after the fact, their assessments are cold and logical, the opposite of the ad war that we see. They agree on each side's strengths and weaknesses and understand the opposition's strategy as exactly what they would do confronted by the same facts.

Do ads work? We have remarkably little knowledge of an answer to that simple question. The professionals prove their belief in them by spending vast sums of money. In a contested election one candidate always wins and the ads get some of the credit. But we don't know whether they should. We have no counterfactual, no case where Smith versus Jones was contested without paid advertising, so we can't know whether a victory for Smith might have been just as impressive if neither candidate spent a dime. We do have numerous cases where only one side does advertising. Usually, that is the winning side, but we can't know whether it was the case that the ads helped or whether it was just that the expected winner was flush with campaign funds.

We know the limits, and therefore the opportunities. Ads can build images of candidates who begin as unknowns. A blank slate can be filled. For those with a long record in politics, it is less clear that ads can do more than spend contributor's money. When unknowns confront unknowns, campaign ads can have their maximum impact. We see that to be the case, for example, in Senate contests, which often pit a millionaire seeking office for the first time against a field of relatively unknown candidates. The millionaire runs a slick ad campaign, emerges with double, triple, or quadruple the name recognition of opponents, and wins. Ads clearly work in this situation.

Issues matter in campaign ads, but not as a debate about public policy. What matters is to be seen as concerned about public affairs, to be "tough on the issues." Usually this is wholly style, not substance. Candidates, especially if inexperience is a liability, will take specific stands in issue ads. But the goal is to show that the candidate actually has thought about public policy, has a plan for governing. Ads that say "strong on issues" are unlikely to convince in the absence of some specifics. So the issue ads should be seen as illustrations, opportunities for the candidate to demonstrate mastery over some subject the public does not know, probably in most cases also one the public does not particularly care about. In ads everything is image. And so the issue ads are just another facet of image. While we might think it desirable for ads to clarify candidate positions on contentious matters, winning is the goal of those who pay for them, and winning is not likely to be enhanced by taking stances that will offend some voters.

Political Science

There is in political science a standard position on many questions, a consensus of scholarship. Presidential campaigns is not one of them. This question, it would surprise those outside the field, is one rarely visited and one on which there is too little work for a standard vision to arise. The explanation is in essence that political science studies "voting" but not elections.[6] Voting is studied by surveys that take place both before (September and October) and after presidential elections. Rich in ability to distinguish between individuals and to account for the motivations that lead some to vote one way and others another, the standard work in political science is impoverished in ability to say anything about campaigns, sequences of events understood to take place over the election year.

The influence of campaigns is best studied in the aggregate, by watching sentiment change over the course of the election season. Political science deals mainly in analysis of individual behavior. Studying individuals over time, though possible, engages difficult and costly research design issues, and so is rarely attempted.

The question raised by political scientists would astonish both the working journalists and the campaign professionals. It is "Do campaigns matter, *at all*?"[7] What everybody else observes is movement, usually huge movements, in the polls during the campaign. Surely, that is a response to the campaign on the road – or to the ad war. What political scientists observe (see Gelman and King 1993) is that after all that movement the outcome ends up being about where it would have been expected to be many, many months before the fact.

---

[6] But for exceptions, see Holbrook 1996 and Campbell 2000.
[7] The question "Do campaigns matter?" is the title of Thomas Holbrook's book on this very subject.

Here is the scenario. Economists and political scientists forecast election outcomes from data that can be known before the campaign begins. (Indicators of the state of the national economy dominate such forecasts.) Although they misforecast the winner of close elections sometimes, on average these forecasts are impressively accurate. If the forecasts say, for example, 52 percent Democratic, then the real outcome is likely to be between 50 and 54. This, we see below, is just slightly inferior to what the polls can predict from the day before the election is held, after the full impact of the campaign.

So, what is the problem? The problem is that accurate forecasts that precede the campaign seem to leave no possibility that the campaign itself actually mattered. The logic is simple. If the campaign mattered, it should have altered the outcome from the pre-campaign forecasts. It didn't. Therefore, campaigns don't matter. If this logic is correct, then nothing that happened between April and the end of October mattered, not the campaign on the road, not the ads, not the candidate debates, not the party conventions, nothing. So goes the story. It seems airtight.

If that story were true, we should see it in the polls. If 52 it was destined to be, then the polls should show 52, more or less (and with the usual random errors from sampling), all the way between forecast and Election Day. They don't. Instead, we see patterns where one candidate seems to have and hold a lead for long periods of time. Then the other surges and in turn holds onto a lead for weeks and months. And then, the polls come back on Election Day to where they were supposed to be all along. So we have a strange result. Something that went on between April and November moved voter sentiment, but always it moved in an eerily predictable direction, coming home to the predicted margin as if drawn by a magnet.

So, campaigns move voters, but how they will move them can be predicted before they begin. That's what the evidence says. I hope the reader shares my consternation at this strange kettle of fish. Gelman and King propose a solution to this puzzle. Campaigns do matter, they say, because although we may know pretty much how things will turn out in March of election years, the voters themselves do not know. They are tuned out of politics, not yet thinking about their eventual evaluative task. They will get plenty of "help" from the parties and candidates, a barrage of persuasion from both sides.

Why, then, does the persuasion lead to a predictable result? The answer is that facts matter. The national economy forms the cleanest case. What state it is actually in is a matter of fact. Employment is high or low.

Inflation is under control or not. Incomes are growing or stagnant. We can cut through all the rhetoric and come to some objective conclusions about these matters. The parties will debate about prosperity, taking predictable sides. Incumbents will say, "Things are great." The opposition will say, "Things could be better." But this debate is not equal. The party with the facts on its side will win the debate. Opinion is not infinitely malleable. When people are feeling prosperous, you can't convince them that they should be depressed. When depressed, messages of economic good cheer fall flat. Facts matter. Voters have independent information about prosperity; they are not dependent on party rhetoric.

So the campaign can be seen as an exercise in information flow. Claims and counterclaims are made and voters listen. The result of the debate becomes predictable precisely because we can know in advance which side will benefit from the debate. It isn't only rhetorical skill. In March, when the accurate forecasts are made, voters have not yet thought about how things are and, more important, how much credit or blame is due the incumbents for it. By the end of the campaign, they become "enlightened" on these matters, reaching conclusions driven in part by the facts used to make the forecasts. Other things are less objective, but the same process goes on for all. Argument meets counterargument, and where some hard evidence is available, the arguments will tend to favor those who have the evidence for their case.

This strikes me as a tortured argument. Its virtue is that no other argument squares with the facts. Now it is time to turn to the horse race, to figure out what is going on in presidential campaigns. I begin with a question newly raised every four years: Do the polls actually predict presidential election outcomes?

DO THE POLLS PREDICT PRESIDENTIAL ELECTIONS?

What makes horse race polls interesting is, inevitably, the belief that they have some ability to predict the outcome of presidential elections. Thus, since the beginning of the sample survey applied to politics, we have been asking, "Do the polls predict the outcome?" It seems a sensible question, and it seems also one that ought to find an answer, "yes" or "no." That we keep on asking decades later begins to suggest that it is less straightforward than it seems, that "yes" and "no" do not exhaust the possibilities.

As in so many other matters, the answer one gets to a question depends on how the question is asked. There are in fact two interesting questions, and the answers will be seen to conflict. Since the beginning of the enterprize pollsters have touted up their final, election-eve numbers and compared them with the national popular vote on the following day. The performance of these "late" predictions is impressive, as we see below. Thus our answer is, "Yes, the polls do predict the election outcome."

The second way to put the question is to ask, "Do the polls predict well when they matter most, which is early in the campaign?" The problem with election eve polls is not that they are wrong; their record is pretty good. The problem is that they don't have much value as information, because you can also get excellent forecasts on election-eve from people on the street. Cab drivers, for example, will tell you who is going to win, and, in my experience, they will be right.[8] The challenge to the polls is to be informative early in the campaign, where foreknowledge of the outcome is scarce. Millions of voters in presidential primaries and caucuses go to the polls thinking about which of their party's candidates is a likely winner in the November election. It matters a lot that the horse race polls on which these strategic judgments are based be right. When we ask how good the forecasts turn out to be, the answer will not be encouraging. We start with the late predictions.

Late Predictions

When pollsters first addressed the accuracy issue, it was the sampling methodology that was in doubt. Naturally, then they used their latest surveys before the election to demonstrate that a sample could predict what many millions of voters would subsequently do. They were testing prediction, that is, not forecasting. By election eve most voters know what they will do and so virtually the only question remaining is whether a sample of them says in a poll turns out to mimic what the voting population will do at the polls.[9]

The simple question "Do the polls predict the outcome?" is actually a bundle of related queries. One is whether the polls call the winner

---

[8] And cab drivers are a refreshing alternative to the spin doctors who give prognostications in the media. Those who drive for a living seem to care more about getting it right than influencing how their listeners should think. The professionals, as a group, are arguably the very worst information source, because the aim of being accurate competes with too many other motivations.

[9] There was – and is – one more issue: whether respondent reports that they intend to go to the polls are predictive of actual behavior. They turn out not to be particularly good; survey respondents considerably overstate voting intentions. That would not be a problem if nonvoters had roughly the same preferences as voters, but often they do not. Determining who are "likely" voters is a thorny problem with no good solution.

correctly. That is what most people care about. But it is not a particu-larly good standard. Outcomes that are very lopsided are no test of the survey method. In elections that are expected to be landslides, you just don't need polls to tell you what everybody already knows. The polls are always right for these cases, but never particularly informative.

The other end of the scale is a different sort of problem. For elections where the outcome is razor-thin, calling the winner correctly is beyond the capability of polls with reasonable sample sizes. In 2000, for example, the final Bush victory of a few hundred votes was determined after a month of recounting the Florida ballots (where differing treatment of contested ballots could have produced a victory for either candidate). Any claim that a poll that could have predicted the final outcome with better than 50–50 odds would have been a fraud. In such a case, where it is impossible to improve on a coin flip, whether or not the polls get it right doesn't reflect either well or badly on the polls.[10]

If calling the winner isn't a suitable standard, we would next turn to asking how close the outcome is to that predicted. By this standard, most of the 2000 polls were right on the mark in saying that the election was too close to call. Individual polls, on average, come within a couple points of calling the outcome right. In recent decades multiple organizations predict the outcome from independent surveys. That improves things a lot. The average of several polls is provably more accurate than any single one – the average essentially is the same as a single survey with many thousand respondents, rather than the smaller numbers in individual polls. Thus the median of surveys on election eve in recent elections is about one point from the actual outcome.[11] All in all, Table 4.1 shows that late predictions from the horse race polls are pretty good.

Early Predictions

Forecasting early in the presidential campaign season is another story altogether. It is useful again to set aside those campaigns where a popular

---

[10] Most survey organizations had George W. Bush leading at the end. But it is worth noting, before too much credit is given or taken, that the national polls predicted the popular vote, narrowly won by Al Gore.

[11] And the pure sampling performance is undoubtedly even better than that, because some of the error is real change, not misprediction. In 2000, for example, the underprediction of Al Gore's vote share is driven by survey respondents who claimed right up to election eve that they would vote for Ralph Nader, but then switched and voted for Gore in the real event.

TABLE 4.1. *The Record of the Polls: Election-Eve Prediction Success*

Year (number of predictions)	Range of prediction (for winner)	Median prediction	Actual winner two-candidate share	Error from median predictions
1952 (1)	51.0	51.0	55.6	−4.6
1956 (1)	59.5	59.5	58.0	1.5
1960 (1)	51.0	51.0	50.0	1.0
1964 (2)	64.0–64.0	64.0	61.0	3.0
1968 (2)	47.7–50.6	49.1	50.0	−0.9
1972 (3)	61.0–65.9	62.0	61.6	0.4
1976 (3)	49.5–52.3	50.5	51.0	−0.5
1980 (4)	50.6–53.8	52.3	55.4	−3.1
1984 (6)	55.4–64.2	59.2	59.0	0.2
1988 (5)	52.1–56.0	54.7	53.5	1.2
1992 (5)	54.3–57.0	55.0	53.8	1.2
1996 (10)	54.4–60.2	56.7	54.4	2.3
2000 (10)	47.4–51.1	48.9	50.0	−1.1

Source: Compiled from National Council on Public Polls.

incumbent is seeking a second term (1956, 1964, 1972, 1984, 1996). The early polls are right in these cases, but the outcomes could have been (and were) correctly forecasted a year or two in advance.

The other campaigns are a different story altogether. With but a single exception – Eisenhower in 1952 – what marks all of them is that every winner would have been predicted to have lost at some point earlier in the campaign year. In all of these more normal, more competitive, presidential elections, the two-party divisions of the intended vote cross over the line in which the candidates divide the votes in two. Of course, every loser would have been predicted to have lost at some early point also. The important point is that early presidential horse race polls are not much better than a coin flip. They are wrong almost as often as they are right.

It is tempting to dismiss the technology of the sample survey as just incapable of measuring vote intentions. Such claims are often made, pretty often by candidates on the wrong end of the current prediction. But we already know from the excellent performance of the pollsters on election eve that the horse race can be predicted very well indeed with this same survey technology.

Why then are the early polls so often wrong? The straightforward answer, one preferred by the working press, is simply that voters changed their minds. The common sort of story is that A was leading B in June and July, but then B put on a good campaign and pulled ahead. That fits the data and fits the focus on what goes over the airwaves from day to day.

It doesn't fit so well what we know about campaigns and, more important, what we know about voters. So accustomed are we to explanations of success and failure in terms of "running a good (or bad) campaign" that it is hard to argue the alternative, that all campaigns are pretty good. But Gelman and King (1993) make the case well. Campaigns are run by candidates, almost invariably proven political winners before they achieve a presidential nomination and by proven professionals in other capacities, such as strategy, advertising, and polling. Furthermore, the huge flow of money into American politics guarantees that even the least promising campaign will have money to spend on everything that might conceivably matter. We don't, for example, see presidential campaigns where one side makes heavy ad buys and other does not; both sides buy furiously.

We do see the *appearance* that one campaign is working and the other is not. In situations where voters decide many months, or even years, in advance, it often appears that the losing candidate is floundering, trying this and that, when nothing works. Often when popular presidents seek reelection we see this scenario. The eventual winner seems calm and effective, pursuing a strategy planned long in advance. The eventual loser seems to have no strategy, trying this and that and finding that nothing works. A phrase from 1996 captures the feeling. Dole "could not get traction," it was said. What is important to realize is that losing candidates, *because they are losing*, have to gamble, have to try out any theme that might possibly work. When down by ten or twenty points with thirty or sixty days to go, a candidate can't just stick to the program; evidence is abundant that the current program will produce a big loss.

What we know about voters also doesn't fit this story. One of the best established findings in voting research is that voters rarely hold a preference for a candidate and then change it to the opponent. Such rare behavior cannot account for the huge swings often observed in the horse race polls.

What then is left? To begin to find an answer, we must take seriously the huge numbers of respondents in surveys of all kinds who say they haven't paid attention, haven't thought about it, don't really have any views, and so forth. What we know from pressing them to say something anyhow is that they are surely telling the truth. We can and do engage in the practice of pressing for a response. Survey firms routinely prompt these nonrespondents to say how they might "lean" after they have claimed no preference. But we have learned that these reluctant responses are almost wholly disorderly. Unlike real responses, they can't be predicted by other things we know about a person's attributes and attitudes.

Attempting to explain why large numbers of survey respondents appeared inconsistent, even contradictory, when asked the same question at different times, Philip Converse (1964) introduced the concept of "nonattitudes." A nonattitude is a survey response made up on the spot during the interview by a respondent who truly has no attitude. Pressed to say *something* by the interviewer, normal people will just make it up. Since these "doorstep opinions" are wholly meaningless to the respondent, the same question at different times will produce different answers.

It needs to be emphasized that nonattitudes are not merely weak or partially formed attitudes. Those who read this book – a group of people whose knowledge of and interest in politics will be highly atypical – will find it strange that large numbers of Americans are totally tuned out of politics most of the time, but that is the case. Asking many people whether, "if the election were held today," they would prefer say George W. Bush or Al Gore is like asking nonflyers whether they prefer the 747 to the 757, asking nonfans about two current baseball players. All these questions can be posed. It is interpreting the answers that gets us into trouble.

If you really don't know or care about a political campaign, how would you answer the horse race question? Randomness is one possibility, and one that is also relatively harmless. But if one name is easy to pronounce and the other hard, why struggle with the hard one? And if one is familiar and the other strange, then in a sense the familiar is easier. And if nothing else matters, the first name mentioned is likely to be the winner. These trivial but systematic factors will leave an imprint on the polls, especially the early polls when large numbers of voters have not yet become engaged in the campaign. When the campaign begins to engage real attitudes, often about in the July–August period of the party conventions, then these trivial factors will melt away. But when they do, they will produce the false appearance of change.

We can now summarize why the early polls forecast poorly. The early polls don't measure real attitudes. What they often tap is a response that was created to satisfy the needs of the interviewer. Later, when replaced by a real attitude, it will appear to have changed. But it really changed from nothing to something. And the problem isn't the polls (or at least isn't the technology of the sample survey); it is the respondents. Polls can't measure what doesn't exist.

SO, WHAT REALLY MATTERS?

We just can't help ourselves. We see a new number every day, often several, then unavoidably we look for an explanation for why it is higher or lower than yesterday. "What happened?" we ask. And we look for some "event," some cause to which we can ascribe effect. And nearly always we are dead wrong. The observed movement turns out to be (1) not real movement, just day-to-day fluctuation, or (2) real movement having nothing to do with the events of the last few days.

It helps to stand back for perspective. When the campaign is long over, looking at those loops and whirls leads to a different understanding, one that emphasizes movements and trends, not good days and bad days. The polls reflect a running tally of everything that matters, most of which will be unrelated to campaign events. Working out what matters is the task of the next section.

We will ask, "Do campaigns matter?" and expect to answer the query with a demonstration that they do or do not move sentiment a point or two or three at the margin. We now know that most of the outcome is fixed before the campaign begins, before even the moment when candidates are selected. This obviously is different from the press or ad war perspectives, which claim more massive effects. But one or two or three points at the margin is no small thing, either. About a third of our presidential elections are close enough that such a shift can change the outcome. A tenth of that could have reversed the 1960 or 2000 presidential squeakers.

The Course of the Campaign

It's time to look at data, specifically, the year-long tracks of the head-to-head contest of the two eventual nominees of the major parties. We have a sufficient density of such polls for the elections since about 1960 to permit detailed analyses. For some purposes, a larger set, dating back to 1952, can be employed.

The polls begin early in the election year, as soon as pollsters figure out what the eventual pairing is likely to be. When the early leading contenders actually win their parties' nomination, the polls can begin even before the election year. In some years, such as 1976, one of the nominees becomes known only after a lengthy primary season, in which case the polls don't start until the nominee attains front-runner status.

To see presidential contest dynamics it is helpful to separate presidential elections into two fundamental categories. One of these, most elections,

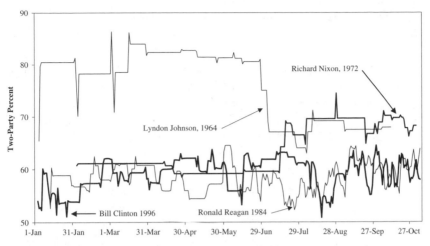

FIGURE 4.1. Four incumbents easily reelected, 1964, 1972, 1984, and 1996.

involves genuine uncertainty about the eventual winner. These are the interesting cases. Another set is quite different.

Reelection Landslides

When incumbent presidents seek a second term and the public is generally satisfied, then the contest is quite different. In such cases the incumbent is easily reelected. Looking beneath the polls we see a different pattern, one in which the public decides at least tentatively to continue the president in office and never becomes engaged in the contest. For many voters it would appear that the decision is not "which candidate is best?" but "does the president deserve another four years?" When the latter question is the focus, voters can tune out the opponent.

Four of those incumbent reelections are seen in Figure 4.1.[12] What characterizes all of them is relative constancy. The first poll of January predicts the eventual outcome about as well as those on the eve of the election, as if nothing that intervened mattered at all. The public we see in Johnson versus Goldwater in 1964, Nixon versus McGovern in 1972, Reagan versus Mondale in 1984, and Clinton versus Dole in 1996 evidently decided to vote for the winner long before the campaign began

---

[12] Here and in subsequent figures I display the winner's share of the two-party vote, not the absolute share. That has two advantages. First, it doesn't make the impressiveness of the winner's share depend on whether or not some third- or fourth-party candidate ran a serious campaign. Second, the two-party vote better maps onto the Electoral College vote on the assumption that the major parties will share all of the electoral votes.

and never reconsidered. This is consistent with the idea that the decision is *for* the incumbent, not *between* incumbent and challenger. We have much commentary, that focuses on these four challengers, asserting that they were peculiarly inept, that their messages were rejected. I think that is wrong in all four cases. What was inept about the four is that they ran against popular incumbents seeking a second term. Replace any of the four with a leading figure from their party and I believe that we would have observed the same four results. That's all we need to know about them.

What is critical in all these four cases is the absence of contest, that the challenger is not taken seriously. It must have been frustrating for each of them to try to craft a message that worked when the public, having already decided to reelect the incumbent, had no interest in their message. We confuse futility with ineptness in these cases. Equally, I think we overestimate the appeal of the incumbents. They seem so formidable, almost superhuman, in these runaway reelections, that we come to think they have patented electoral magic. But it isn't magic. It is simply the public saying, in essence, "They've had four years and things aren't too bad, so they deserve another four."[13] To get a sense of their real limitations, it is notable that all four suffered public rejection after their landslide victories. The reasons involve events of huge magnitude, Vietnam for Johnson, Watergate for Nixon, the Iran-Contra scandal for Reagan, the Lewinsky scandal for Clinton. But four out of four is still telling.

These cases – and Eisenhower versus Stevenson in 1956 if we had better data – are good evidence for the "campaigns don't matter" thesis. Nothing that happened during the election year seems to have altered their outcomes. Lest that conclusion seem too obvious, it is noteworthy that each has been the subject of many books that tell riveting stories of how key events changed history. And we can't say for sure that they are wrong. Maybe the victories only seemed inevitable. What we can say is that the outcomes could have been predicted from the politics of the previous November, long before the hoopla began. Thankfully, most presidential elections are more interesting. I turn to them now.

Contested Elections

The six closely contested elections I divide into two sets for graphical convenience. Like the previous set, the track displayed is that of the eventual

---

[13] We can be more specific about "things aren't so bad." Presidents who have above-average real income growth are always reelected when they seek a second term (Erikson et al. 2002, pp. 244–45.) Although things must be a bit more complicated, this simple predictor cleanly divides the available cases into winners and losers.

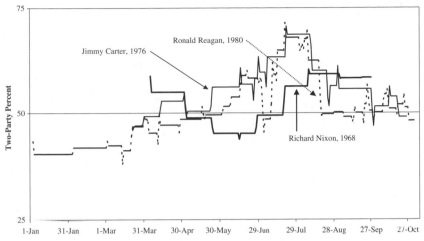

FIGURE 4.2. Three campaign tracks: 1968, 1976, and 1980.

(popular vote) winner. The first three, Nixon versus Humphrey in 1968, Carter versus Ford in 1976, and Reagan versus Carter in 1980, are displayed in Figure 4.2. Two patterns are notable in both sets of three. One is that unlike the stagnant contests just seen, there is a great deal of systematic movement over the election year. The polls move over a range that is considerably larger than ever seen in actual outcomes. Another is that in every case winners were behind at some point in the election year. The polls say that every one of these outcomes would have been opposite if elections were held in April, May, or June instead of November.

Figure 4.3 displays the tracks for the three more recent contested elections, Bush versus Dukakis in 1988, Clinton verus Bush in 1992, and Gore versus George W. Bush in 2000.[14] The visual difference between the two figures reflects the abundance of data for the recent elections. This I presume is how the others would look if hundreds of polls had been available for those cases as they are for recent elections. The slightly smaller range of movement partly reflects better data.[15]

As with the first set, the intriguing fact of these three contests is that all winners came from behind. Other than incumbents, it seems politics is like NASCAR; it's best to be in second place going into the last lap.

[14] The track is the Gore percentage of the two-party division, so far as I can tell about the only benefit of winning the popular vote.
[15] Sampling theory predicts that more extreme cases – those, say, four or five points too positive or too negative – will be observed in relatively thin data series. For recent elections they have lesser influence because they are averaged together with normal readings on the same days.

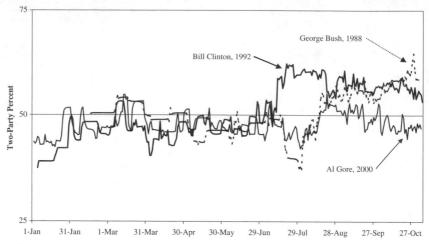

FIGURE 4.3. Three campaign tracks: 1988, 1992, and 2000.

Before we can properly appreciate how much real change is going on in these data, we need to come to terms with these jiggly lines and what they mean.

These daily compilations of the polls are still not a clean picture of reality. We know from sampling theory that each poll is a combination of measured reality and error. Each will capture more or less the true standing of the candidates. But along with that standing each will have error, typically in the neighborhood of two points. The problem with survey error is that although we know *that* there is error, we don't know *what* it is. If we have George W. Bush at, say, 51 percent, the true number might be only 49 or might be 53. These errors arise from pure chance, from sampling one group of, say, 1,000 people on a particular day instead of another, chosen by equally arbitrary and random processes.

From a single poll the problem of separating measure from error is hopeless. But when we put polls into a series we have some ability to begin to separate the two. Begin with an assumption that opinion moves smoothly, that millions of people do not change their minds from one day to the next. We have a good deal of evidence to support such an assumption. Thus day-to-day blips are probably just that, blips. If the change were real, it would persist. If George W. Bush's standing goes from 51 to 53 on a particular day, and then stays in that neighborhood for several days and in several polls, then we have probably seen real change. But that same two-point increase followed by return back to where it was in subsequent polls pretty clearly indicates sampling error.

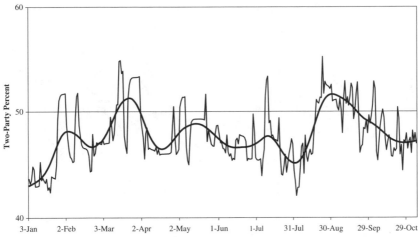

FIGURE 4.4. The 2000 horse race: percent for Gore (smooth approximation in bold).

That intuition about persistence suggests that we should eliminate one-day and one-poll movements, but keep evidence of longer, multiple day, movements. We need a method to observe the smooth underlying movement that we believe underlies the noisy series of horse race polls. There are several smoothing techniques that serve this purpose. All of them have in common that they retain evidence of persistent movements and smooth over mere blips.

One of these is illustrated for Al Gore's percentage of the 2000 race in Figure 4.4.[16] Notice that the smooth line captures all of what looks real in the full-year contest. A picture of how the polls differ from the smooth line would look like pure randomness, up and down daily movements without pattern of any kind. The smooth line, in contrast, moves. Its movements beg for explanation. That explanation will come from politics, not merely the technology of the sample survey.

Does it matter whether we look at the numbers themselves or estimate their underlying movements? It does. Look at the last month or so of the campaign. The numbers say that three times Al Gore pulled ahead of Bush, all three times then falling back quickly. Gore could grab a lead but he couldn't hold it, one might say. The smooth line, in contrast, says, "nonsense"; those three "leads" were statistical illusions. Gore didn't lose

[16] The method employed is the Hodrick-Prescott filter (Hodrick and Prescott 1980), a method that emphasizes low-frequency movements and penalizes high-frequency movements.

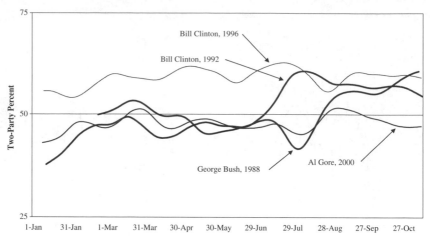

FIGURE 4.5. Variation in the campaigns of 1988, 1992, and 2000.

leads because he never had them.[17] If we believe the raw numbers, we'll go looking for events that explain Gore's surges and declines. If we believe the smooth estimate – and I do – then those searches for explanation will be fruitless. Random fluctuation is beyond explanation. What we can't do is search for the daily events that appear to explain the pattern, because we will always find them. Something happens every day in a presidential campaign. If the surges are completely artifactual, just sampling variation, we will still find candidate events that appear to explain them.

Figure 4.5 illustrates the effect of smoothing. It portrays the three campaigns of Figure 4.3, adding the Clinton-Dole 1996 contest for reference. The Clinton 1996 campaign is a strong case for "campaigns don't matter." Not a perfectly flat line, it nonetheless doesn't go anywhere. It is hard to ascribe causal significance to movements that don't cumulate and don't last. But that sets up a standard for the other three, which now show dramatic movement. Purged of the random error, these three campaigns show about as much systematic movement as it is possible to imagine. These are real horse races, right to the final stretch. The campaigns of Figure 4.2 – 1960, 1968, and 1976 – probably would look similar if we had the density of polling in those years that we have for recent elections. Their more "jumpy" tracks come from movements between infrequent

---

[17] Recall that the polls are probably biased by about two points against Gore in 2000 due to voters who claimed that they would support Ralph Nader, but were actually closet Gore voters when it mattered. So when I say that Gore was never ahead in the last month, I mean ahead in the polls. In reality he might have been ahead.

polls and from the enhanced effect of random fluctuation on small series.

What we now know is that there is room for campaigns to matter, and to matter a lot. That points to events that happen along the way as possible explanations. I turn now to an analysis of two of the repeatable kind, nominating conventions and candidate debates.

Much of what goes on in presidential campaigns that might matter is idiosyncratic, particular historical events such as the Iran hostage crisis. However much they might matter, there is no systematic way to observe their influence. But every campaign has nominating conventions and most have candidate debates. Those repeatable phenomena can be observed.

PARTY NOMINATING CONVENTIONS

At the dawn of the television age in the early 1950s, which is pretty much the dawn of serious political polling as well, presidential nominating conventions were raucous affairs, uncontrolled and unpredictable. Americans could tune in their snowy black and white televisions and see history happening in front of them. And they did tune in. An electorate normally tuned out and uninterested found the conventions pretty interesting and exciting, the Olympic games of politics. There were memorable calls of the states as the conventions fought over rules, platforms, and candidates.

That kind of citizen interest is so strikingly different from normal that one would expect the experience to carry influence. Just the time spent matters. Citizen attention to politics varies across the full scale from "political junkie" to nothing. But for some, the three or four evenings in front of the TV set represent as many hours thinking about politics as occur in the four-year span between conventions. We expect change of attitudes to occur when people are actually focused on politics, and this is the focal event.

Nominating conventions by the end of the twentieth century were anything but raucous. Convention managers had learned that the conventions, if run smoothly, could have big positive effects on the campaign. In the case of the Democrats, the 1968 convention riots also illustrated the harm that could come from out-of-control expression. Hubert Humphrey's campaign for the presidency never recovered from the events of four days of street battles between antiwar protesters and police.[18]

---

[18] My earlier speculation that conventions are particularly important for a "coming out" of former vice presidents into a new public image is richly consistent with the 1968

Coupled with the multiplication and progressively earlier staging of state presidential primaries, the element of unpredictability was lost. In 2000, for example, both George W. Bush and Al Gore had solid majorities of committed delegates in early March, four to five months before the conventions were staged. For many years the conventions were still a good show as fights over the party platform or the vice presidential nominee replaced selecting the presidential nominee as the main events. Those too are now gone. Unfortunately for TV viewers, convention managers have learned that control makes for good TV impression. The impulse to have a good fight is now effectively suppressed by managers who want no interruptions of the unplanned in their scripted shows. Boring works.

As the conventions become ever more boring and predictable, TV coverage has fallen off and viewership has declined. The opportunity to see history being made is gone. The conventions merely ratify what has long been known, long ago decided. Nonetheless, the practices that have emerged over how the conventions are staged, how the attention is focused on one party in its special week, how the opposition goes quiet (convention week is normally scheduled as a vacation break for the other party's campaign), and how the media commentators limit their skepticism while the show is going on all continue. So even as the public loses interest, it is possible that a party's convention could still produce a "bounce" for its candidate's team.

The net effect of the two conventions must, on average, be zero. Since both parties hold conventions, whatever their typical effects, the effects should be offsetting. Perhaps that accounts for the scarcity of analysis of their effects. But that is true only on average. In a particular campaign the possibility exists that one side may get a bigger bounce than the other, and hence a prospect that the convention bounce might matter for the outcome.

Because the two conventions in each campaign are at least partially offsetting, it is hard to see a clean picture of the effects. Party A holds its convention and gains a few points. Then two or three weeks later B stages a convention and wins back the momentum that A had earlier gained. To get a sense of how much the conventions matter, I am going to assess only the second one for each campaign, the one case where we can see effects over several weeks that do not get canceled.

result. Instead of Hubert Humphrey, what 1968 convention viewers saw was Richard J. Daley, mayor of Chicago, the Chicago police at their low point, and antiwar demonstrators. There was a lot of action packed into those four days, but none of it was any good for Humphrey.

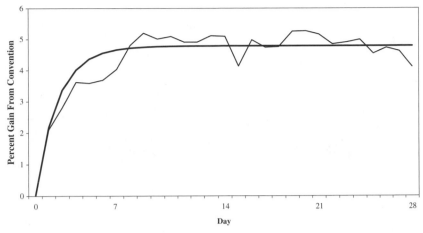

FIGURE 4.6. Effect of the second party convention over twenty-eight days: daily estimates (smoothed effect in bold)

Timing of the nominating conventions is not arbitrary. By custom, the "out" party always goes first. The party that currently holds the White House then follows some weeks later. The span between the two varies from almost nothing (1956) to the more typical two or three weeks to six weeks (1972). It doesn't appear to matter which goes first. The thirteen elections divide into six first convention winners, six second convention winners, and, for harmony, the thirteenth case, a virtual tie in which the first convention party won the electoral vote and the second won the popular vote.

To assess the convention impact on the party that holds it I estimated the gain in the party's share of the horse race polls for each of twenty-eight days following the opening of the convention.[19] The four-week period is chosen to provide the lengthiest period postconvention that does not entangle the summer convention effects with fall campaigning and debates. That effect is displayed in Figure 4.6 along with a smooth estimate of the convention effect that summarizes the twenty-eight independent estimates.

Two things are notable about the effect. One is that it is very large. The almost five-point impact of the convention is nearly as much net movement as we have seen in the previous figures for a whole campaign. Second, it is permanent. A full four weeks after the convention, the effect

[19] Because most survey respondents would be interviewed before the opening gavel on the evening of day one, the impact is assessed beginning on the first day after the opening.

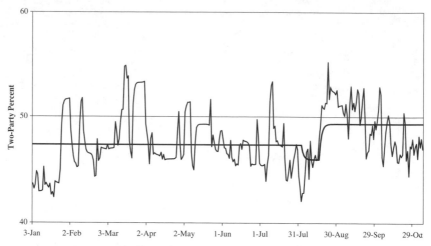

FIGURE 4.7. Estimated effect of two-party nominating conventions on the 2000 campaign: actual percent for Gore and estimated convention effects.

has not decayed at all. Often called the convention "bounce," this effect is clearly misnamed. Things that bounce go up and then come back down. The convention effect goes up and, the evidence says, stays up.

The idea of a bounce no doubt comes from observing both conventions. The effect of the first never lasts because it is promptly offset by the second. But what these data say is that the temporary appearance of the first is an illusion. It is really a permanent gain for the first party that is later offset by a permanent loss of about the same magnitude when the second party holds its convention. This distinction matters. A true "bounce" would be transient, an effect in polls for a few days that would have been long gone by election day. A permanent effect means that the party that gets the better bounce – and things are never exactly equal – will carry that advantage into the election.

Consider the Bush versus Gore campaign of 2000. What can we say about the effect of the nominating conventions on this squeaker? Almost anything could have changed the 2000 outcome; the list of possibilities would be long and not very meaningful. So we need to impose a higher standard. Could it have materially changed?

It is possible to estimate the contribution of the two conventions in 2000.[20] The estimated effects, seen in Figure 4.7, show the Democratic

---

[20] The size of the convention bounce is estimated by imposing the standard shape from Figure 4.6 on the horse race standings and estimating for each case whether it expands

convention to have had about double the net effect of the earlier Republican gathering. This flies in the face of general agreement among commentators that the Republican convention was a better political show than the Democratic version. But this effect captures actual shifts from Bush to Gore in the polls. It is not an artistic judgment. Combining the estimates of the small Republican bounce and the larger Democratic one, I come up with an estimate that the net effect is about two points (more precisely, 2.001). Removing those two points moves Al Gore from his predicted 49.35 percent share – an underestimate of the actual 50.27 percent of the final (two-party) vote that he got – down to 47.35 percent.

How important is the two-point effect? Well, history would have been very different without it. As always, talking about "points" in a poll leads to underestimating importance. First, instead of narrowly winning the popular vote, Gore would have cleanly lost it by almost two million votes. Second, take two points off his Florida totals and there would have been no controversy, no need to recount. But Florida would not have mattered, anyway. Take two points off each of Gore's state totals and he also loses Iowa, New Mexico, Oregon, and Wisconsin, the sum of which, thirty electoral votes, put him too far out of reach for Florida's twenty-five to matter. The convention effect matters.

The convention effect in 2000 is far from the largest asymmetry. In 1992 Clinton and Gore put on an upbeat feel-good show that energized the Democratic party for a sprint to the finish. The Republicans that year featured angry speeches about "family values" that did not play well at all. The result was a decisive edge to the Democrats, by my estimate the biggest differential ever, accounting for ten points of Bill Clinton's final margin. That is a good deal larger than Clinton's win (53.4 to 46.6).

Only slightly smaller is the historic 1968 campaign, where the contrast between a united Republican show nominating Richard Nixon produced a better than average bounce, while the Democrats featured the most closely covered street riots of all times. The mob of press and television in Chicago for the Democratic convention quickly refocused on the angry confrontations between demonstrators and Chicago police. The demonstrators featured the angriest and most unkempt, to whom the TV cameras naturally migrated. The Chicago police and their boss, Mayor Richard

or shrinks to fit the actual data for the period after both conventions. In 2000, for example, Republicans get a factor of .29, which multiplies the full effect of almost five points, and Democrats get .71. So both parties have smaller than average (1.0) bounces, but the Democratic bounce produces the two-point relative gain when all the arithmetic is done.

J. Daley, were a low point in modern law enforcement, appearing more intent on doing bodily damage to demonstrators than on keeping order. Hubert Humphrey, the "Happy Warrior," was left to try to run a campaign while an angry nation debated which side of the street riots it liked least. Humphrey had to try to explain how the Democrats, who couldn't organize a peaceful gathering to nominate a candidate, would be able to run the country. He didn't succeed. The convention effect I estimate was worth 7.8 points to Richard Nixon, which is about 6.8 more than needed to win the election.

Nixon also benefited from the contrast in 1972, but didn't need the edge in that contest. The Democrats put on the last of the anything-goes, uncontrolled conventions in that year, managing to start late and fill prime time with lengthy speeches and floor fights while George McGovern's acceptance speech, the key opportunity to get attention from voters, was pushed to 3 A.M., virtually early morning the day after. The size of his audience must have rivaled the numbers who heard acceptance speeches before the dawn of mass communications. The year 1988 is the other case of really decisive convention influence. This time there was no such obvious culprit on the Democratic side. Perhaps the party just lacked enthusiasm. The contrast was important. A close race going into the convention, Michael Dukakis got a typical bounce from the Democratic convention. George Bush got more than twice as much from the Republican convention, moving him into a lead that he held through Election Day.

The conclusion that emerges from this analysis is simple. Party nominating conventions are very important, a key influence on winning and losing. Compared with other things, which are small, scattered, often offsetting, conventions are the key thing. But what is it exactly about a nominating convention that has such influence?

The Causality of the Bounce

What we know for sure, all we know for sure, about the convention effects is when they occur. We call them convention bounces because systematic movements in the polls tend to happen during and shortly after the conventions meet. If something else is happening at about the same time, then perhaps the conventions get too much credit. But there are no good candidates for that "something else" role.

The data are clear. In every contest since 1972 (which is to say, in every contest for which we have good data), the winner gained ground when his own party met and lost ground when the opposition met. All the way back to 1960, indeed, that pattern is broken by only one exception, in 1972. Richard Nixon, on his way to a landslide win, gained ground while the Democrats met to nominate McGovern. Something was going on. But what?

Why do the conventions have such big effects? The reasons are numerous. One is that they energize the faithful. Most partisans in the United States are willing to stray, to find the other party's candidates engaging or their programs attractive. What the conventions can do is remind them why they are on one side and not the other, to reinforce emotional and symbolic ties. Democrats in 1980 who were Poles or Lithuanians and union members found Ronald Reagan, with he-man image, optimism, and engaging smile, an attractive figure. But if they tuned in the Democratic convention of that year, they saw delegates who had Polish and Lithuanian names, and union members wearing bowling shirts with the name of the union local written on the backs. Firming up the party base is easier to do than convincing the other side, or even neutrals, and usually pays bigger dividends in votes. Hence conventions prominently feature appeals to pure partisanship, reminders of common values and memories of past candidates and campaigns. Four days of that symbolic appeal exert a powerful pull on those who tune in.

Conventions also unite the party factions. Many conventions occur after bruising intraparty battles over the nomination, where the losing side has reason not to like the nominee, not to be engaged or supportive of the campaign. Conventions are an opportunity for winners, enlisting their beaten opponents as allies, to reach out to the losing side and say, "We are all Republicans" (or Democrats). The 1980 Republican convention was particularly crucial in that regard. Ronald Reagan, although a fixture in Republican politics since the 1960s, was an outsider, his campaign an insurgency against Republican regulars, with whom he had jousted four years earlier, trying to unseat Gerald Ford. Had he not successfully healed the rift, starting with the choice of George Bush for the vice presidency, he could not have been successful in November.

We don't know very well who moves when the polls move. I surmise that much of the convention bounce is from partisans of these sorts, the uninvolved who might have strayed and the involved on the losing side of primary campaigns. Both have reason to say they will not support the party's candidate before the convention and both have reason to change, to come home to the comfortable associations of the past. We tend to think of campaigns and polls as a struggle for the undecided and the independents. But given how little interest those groups show in politics, they are not particularly likely to respond to conventions.

For the undecided, if they tune in – a very big "if" these days – they will be exposed to about twelve hours of unpaid political advertising. Increasingly scripted by advertising professionals, the conventions are the party's best opportunity to get out a wholly one-sided message. Some of this is the building or rebuilding of image. Voters who tuned into the Democratic convention in 2000 might have believed that Al Gore was born wearing a blue suit with his finger pointing in the air debating public issues. The convention was an opportunity to humanize Gore, to show that indeed he had a childhood and youth, had served in Vietnam, was a person. George Bush (the elder) accomplished the same thing, more successfully the data say. The rap on Bush was that he was a "wimp," a nearly meaningless but nonetheless pejorative term. The real George Bush, anything but wimp-like, had been an athlete in his youth, a courageous fighter pilot in the Pacific war against Japan. Little was heard of the "wimp factor" after the Republican convention.

Things that the parties do are not the whole story. Even if their shows were uninspired and ineffective they would still benefit from two customs. One of these is that the press changes its usual behavior during the conventions. Acting as if they were household guests, not the usual curmudgeons, reporters aren't quite as critical as usual. Not wholly uncritical, they still are somewhat restrained about calling the party message a pack of lies. We know that whether or not the press is a neutral arbiter, the public counts on it to play that role, to tell voters which interpretation is more plausible when the parties disagree. To the extent that criticism is restrained, the party holding the convention gains a temporary advantage.

The parties benefit also from absence of opposition. Following custom, the other party does not schedule important campaign events during the convention. Often the other party convention is the occasion for a vacation from the hectic pace of the year-long campaign. These four-day periods, and perhaps a day or two before and after, represent the only one-sided campaigning we see. One party puts out its message without the usual countermessage. This too should produce a bounce, although only a temporary one.

Some Long-term Patterns

Looking at fifty years of data, some general conclusions emerge. First, it appears to be the case that maximum convention bounces occurs for candidates who are not well known. For them the convention is the opportunity to fill an empty image with positive content. Image, we know, can be built for a candidate who is unknown, but is very hard to change for someone the public knows well. For candidates who ran twice, for example, the convention bounce for their first run is more than twice that of the second, even though they were more likely to win the reelection bid and by bigger numbers. Look for conventions to matter most when an unknown challenger, for example, Bill Clinton in 1992, takes on a well-known opponent. In these cases the challenger is likely to come from behind and to gain the advantage at convention time.

Republicans have done about 30 percent better on average than Democrats. That probably is not an enduring advantage, but just a reflection of the two Democratic disaster conventions of 1968 and 1972, in 1972 when all the action was after midnight and 1968 when the Democrats wished it had been. Excluding those two cases, the party bounces are near identical on average.

My bottom line on the conventions is that they are times of intense political learning. A public that is nearly always tuned out tunes in for a few days, and those are opportunities to learn about people and programs, times to change views. The more there is to learn – when candidates are unknown or suffer from inaccurate images, as do vice presidents – the more important the occasion. Nothing else in campaigning compares.

When we look back at campaigns, and particularly when we do so through the lens of television, we are most apt to remember the candidates standing together on stage in the TV debate. The famous barbs and gaffes make good thirty-second recreations of the feel of an election. But do they matter for the outcome? Are they the moments that turned history? Or are they merely convenient stock footage for story telling?

CANDIDATE DEBATES

Next Tuesday is election day. Next Tuesday all of you will go to the polls, you will stand there and make a decision. I think when you make that decision, it might be well if you would ask yourself: Are you better off than you were four years ago? Is it easier for you to go and buy things in the stores than it was four years ago? Is there more or less unemployment in the Country than there was four years ago? Is America as respected throughout the world as it was? Do you feel that our security is as safe, that we are as strong as we were four years ago? And if you answer all those questions, "Yes," why then I think your choice is very obvious as to who you will vote for [nods toward Jimmy Carter]. If you don't agree, if you don't think that this course that we have been on for the last four years is what you would like to see us follow for the next four, then I can suggest another choice that you have.... [Ronald Reagan, October 29, 1980, from his closing summary]

One of the classic moments of televised presidential debates, Ronald Reagan's challenge to voters to evaluate the last four years hit home. It became a defining characteristic of 1980. The great debates are the source of campaign legend. It was Richard Nixon's bad makeup job in the historic match with John F. Kennedy that made him look sweaty, tense, and untrustworthy. Gerald Ford lost the presidency over a silly claim about Eastern Europe, deflecting a Carter jab that didn't score anyway. Ronald Reagan's joke about opponent Mondale's age was the key moment of the 1984 contest. These have become the standard fare of explaining election outcomes for the presidency. Do they really explain them? Do the debates decide outcomes?

We know the typical scenario and what we know should give us pause about strong interpretations. In the usual case, the polls of debate watchers ask, "Who won?" and return a mixed verdict, about proportional to the candidate's standing in the polls. Morning-after newspaper accounts complain of boredom, bemoan the lack of real action, deny that there could have been a winner. To read them again, years later, is to see how legends are created, for the decisive stories that come to be told don't seem to have been noticed by those writing fresh from just having witnessed the real thing. But some commentator, under the guise of neutrality, declares a winner. Then the polls change. Those who watched the debate didn't agree on a winner. But after the commentator's call, new polls, now including many who did not witness the event, now say by larger numbers that the "winner" won. Eventually, the win becomes fact, it acquires an "everybody knows" status as political legend.

Somebody does win the presidential contest. Having won, we ask why. Why did the winner win? Why did the loser lose? It is tempting to use the debate to settle both questions, to find high moments that were good for the winner and lows that were bad for the loser. The horse race polls are a useful corrective to all this. They, unlike the stories we tell after the fact, are not a social construction. They are what they are. If the debates are as decisive as claimed, we should see the debate winner rise in the polls. To be truly decisive, the rise should be enough to account for the victory margin.

To get a feel for what's going on, we need to see beneath the surface of the polls. For the surface is the roiling waves of sampling fluctuation, the ups and downs of daily movement that mean exactly nothing. The polls rise or fall by a point or two because today's sample of 1,000 citizens is different from yesterday's. We need to know what's happening beneath the waves, whether candidates are gaining or losing momentum.

How Much Influence

Thomas Holbrook (1996), in his careful analysis of the effect of debates in three contests, makes the point that the debates can hardly be as influential as often claimed because they occur so late in the process that most voters have already decided on their candidates. That makes the voters rooters in the debates, cheering for their sides, not dispassionate observers neutrally scoring points. And we also know that not a lot of change occurs in the time span between debates and voting, which can be as short as one week at the extreme. If the eventual winner is already well ahead when the debate is held, claims for debate influence on the outcome are not credible.

We can get a big picture of the issue by looking at when change occurs in candidate standing and when debates are held. For a summary first view, Figure 4.8 combines the polls of the five winners in the closely contested

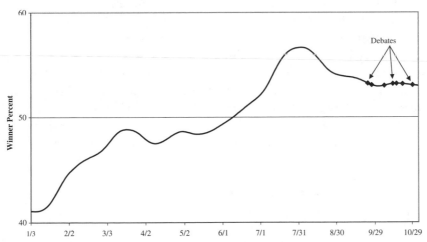

FIGURE 4.8. Winner percent of the two-party intended vote for five contested campaigns (smoothed): 1976, 1980, 1988, 1992, and 2000.

elections of 1976, 1980, 1988, 1992, and 2000 (again treating Gore, the 2000 popular vote winner, as winner). As if they were five versions of one campaign, the polls from each date are averaged together and then the whole thing smoothed to purge it of sampling variation.

This puts the Holbrook timing argument in even stronger light. The figure clearly shows that important things do happen, every eventual winner coming from behind. But those important movements have already happened before the first debate is ever aired. The period in which the debates are going on is actually the flattest in the entire year, the time when change is least apparent.

We know something about why this should be so. Recall the fundamental argument that observed change over the campaign is not people switching from one candidate to another, it is switching by the uninvolved from having no preference at all (but nonetheless answering when pressed to do so in a survey) to having a real preference. After people first think about the contest, first view it on television, first have conversations about it with friends or family, then they come down on one side or the other, where most will stay through election day. When the numbers are showing systematic movement (the point of smoothing being to highlight systematic movement), then people are making decisions. When the movement stops, they have already decided. What the figure clearly shows is that, at least averaged over five campaigns, systematic movement has stopped before the debates are held.

On average the audience for a presidential candidate debate is about half the number of people who will go to the polls. What we know of decisions to participate in politics generally permits a guess about who that half will be. They are much more likely, in the first instance, to be partisans – those who think of themselves as belonging to one of the two major parties – than independents. Either because having chosen sides makes one more interested or because those who are more interested are more likely to take sides, interest in matters political is highly associated with being committed to one side of the party debate. And then, even if one is not partisan, having decided for whom to vote makes the contest more interesting; rooting for a side is more engaging than neutral observation. So, even though we think of the debates as a struggle to influence the undecided, the numbers of undecided viewers should be small.

What we know about late deciders reinforces this view. Far from the editorial page heroes who calmly absorb facts and put off decision until all the facts are in, real late deciders are instead people so totally uninvolved in politics, so little interested, so little informed, that they are barely aware that a presidential campaign is occurring.[21] It is highly improbable that they will tune in to the candidate debates, when most citizens with greater interest in politics do not.

So, the debates occur so late in the process that most voters have already decided, and the audience they attract will consist in the main of loyalists to each side. That doesn't leave much room for influence. But a fair test requires looking at individual contests, where it is possible that some of the effects that are lost in averaging emerge where they matter.

The successful reelection campaigns can be set aside at the outset. With year-long, large leads, debate effects are too late and too small to play a role in these contests. The 1984 campaign is an interesting case that is part exception and part confirmation of the general point. Ronald Reagan's performance in the first debate against Walter Mondale was poor. He didn't seem alert, on top of his game, and seemed at moments confused and dazed. For a man later diagnosed with Alzheimer's disease, it seems possible that we were seeing early symptoms. His big lead did slip in the polls, and it seems possible that a second such performance would have shaken it. The American electorate was prepared to give him another four years, but a whiff of suspicion that he could not do the job might have changed that. In any case the second performance was strong, doubts were erased, and 1984 ended up being another case where debates didn't figure in the outcome.

So we look to the closely contested races for the key evidence that debates might matter. That is seen in Figure 4.9, which pictures the first three campaigns in which televised debates were held, 1960, 1976, and 1980.[22] The first of these is the 1960 squeaker, of which, like the later 2000 campaign, it can be said that *anything* could have altered the outcome. So if we ask whether the debates might have mattered, the answer can only be "yes." But so too it might have mattered if the elections were held on Monday or Wednesday instead of Tuesday. The smoothed horse race polls do show, however, that Kennedy's winning margin did not come from the debates with Nixon. Kennedy was by a trivial amount further ahead on the eve of the famous first debate than in his Election Day margin. And these

---

[21] This should not be misconstrued as an argument about political independents. Independents, like partisans, come from across the span of political knowledge and involvement. The late deciders, in contrast, are distinctly those of least knowledge, interest, and awareness of politics. It takes a powerful amount of noninvolvement not to have chosen sides so late in the game.

[22] There were no debates in 1964, 1968, or 1972.

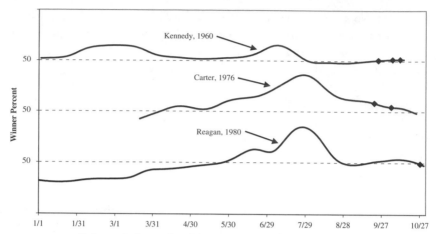

FIGURE 4.9. Debate timing and opinion movement for the 1960, 1976, and 1980 campaigns (smoothed horse race data with diamond symbols indicating debates).

data suggest that the trend that carried him to the finish line originated in late July, two months before the first debate.

Observers of the 1976 debates between Jimmy Carter and Gerald Ford generally gave the nod to Carter. Ford was hurt by his gaffe of claiming at an awkward moment that there was no Soviet influence in Eastern Europe. But if that was the case – that is, if Carter really was the winner – then the debates could have played no role, because Carter lost some of his lead following the debates.

The 1980 campaign is one that might have turned on the last-minute debate. Here the data lead us astray, showing Reagan slipping at the end (in the public polls) when we know from the outcome (and from Carter's polls) that he had to have been moving upward. This is partly a matter of timing. The Carter polls show Reagan pulling ahead in the final two days, after most polling organizations were no longer in the field. Could it be that Reagan's effective line – "Ask yourself if you were better off four years ago" – turned the election? It might have, along with the hostage crisis, changed minds at the final moment. But we need to remember that the stagnating economy was an everyday Reagan theme; it was the problem for which his proposed tax cut was the solution. And, in addition, this was not just a well-turned debate line. The remark was made in a year in which consumer expectations for the economic future reached an all-time low. There was a real economy, real personal experience, that made the debate line work.[23]

[23] This points to the insight of Gelman and King's "enlightenment" theory of the campaign. What the campaign can do that makes it matter is to take facts that people already know

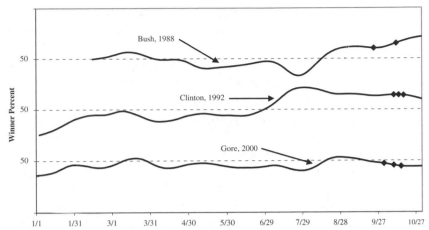

FIGURE 4.10. Debate timing and opinion movement for the 1988, 1992, and 2000 campaigns (smoothed horse race data with diamond symbols indicating debates).

The Bush versus. Dukakis campaign of 1988 was never close after Labor Day (see Fig. 4.10). Bush took a steady lead in the July convention season and held it. His two debates with the colorless Dukakis might have added a point to his margin, but are not needed to explain why he won.

Much the same can be said of the 1992 Clinton campaign. Clinton's lead in the (sometimes) three-candidate race was built during the conventions and never seriously challenged after that. If the debates mattered for the 1992 outcome, then we must declare George Bush their winner, because Bush gained a little ground after the debates.

In the Bush versus Gore 2000 race, like 1960, anything could have changed this outcome, including trivial things. But this campaign is probably the best case for debate influence. Observers of the debates thought Gore soured voters by his aggressive behavior in first debate, going for a knockout punch that he failed to achieve. These judgments are hard to confirm, but this one at least was true enough that Gore changed his style dramatically in subsequent debates. Recalling that Gore's horse race numbers were artificially low because millions of voters told pollsters that they would vote for Ralph Nader, but then voted for Gore, Gore was probably actually ahead on the eve of the debates, and perhaps by a big enough margin that his popular vote win would also have carried the electoral college vote that mattered. Although Gore slipped following the debates,

(e.g., the economy is sour) and translate them into political decisions. Rhetoric alone doesn't work, but rhetoric can serve to connect facts to decisions. And without the rhetoric, the connection might not happen.

his downward trend was in place before the debates were held. This isn't a decisive call for the influence of TV debates, but influence certainly cannot be ruled out, either.[24]

What can we conclude, then, about the debates? What we have seen is perhaps some influence. The evidence is inconclusive to say either that debates matter or that they do not. But if they do matter at all, their influence is vastly smaller than, say, the conventions. The reelection landslides show that once voters have decided, debates will not change the outcome.

There is no case where we can trace a substantial shift to the debates. But in elections that were close at debate times, there are cases (1960, 1980, 2000) where the debates might have been the final nudge. As to why they are so often featured as the central story line of a presidential election campaign, I lean to the idea that they are conveniently available TV footage.

We have seen movements over decades in Chapters 2 and 3, movements over days in this chapter. I turn now from tides and eddies to the waves, movements between elections in which citizens decide to grant or withhold support for those who govern.

---

[24] Mayer (2002) reports a fact that bears on the issue. Isolating "swing voters," those who are essentially neutral in the evaluations they offer in the National Election Studies pre-election surveys of September and October (all or virtually all conducted before the debates), he finds that these voters came out slightly (52%) in Gore's camp. Since they were neutral before the debates and slightly pro-Gore after, there is no debate effect to be found that is pro-Bush, the consensus winner among the pundits.

5

Between the Campaigns

Public Approval and Disapproval of Government

He had famously asked, "Are you better off than you were four years ago?" He had known the answer would be "no." He had said he could do better. Now, in April 1982, Ronald Reagan was in trouble. After a year of relatively good outcomes in 1981, the U.S. economy came full circle, from stagnation to modest growth, and now crashing into full-scale recession. Reagan's early approval ratings had been strong, often in the upper 60s. He had averaged upper 50s. Now as the economy started to slide, so, too, did Reagan's standing. It was low 50s in the fall of 1981 and dropped below 50 briefly in November. After one rebound, it went below 50 and stayed. By April he was at 43. It was not as low as he would go.

Ronald Reagan surely knew the insider's rule of thumb about approval and reelection: Below 50, you lose. Not precise and not based on many cases, the rule of thumb nonetheless had a perfect track record. Voters and consumers had been pessimistic in October 1980, when Reagan had asked, "Are you better off?" Now their pessimism had sunk lower still. Production was declining. The number of unemployed had passed 10 million. After July of his first year in office, when the unemployment rate stood at 7.2 percent, it began to rise, continuing upward every single month. It was reaching near a modern high point at 9.3 in April, from which it would rise into unknown double-digit territory in September. Reagan approval marched in counter step. It reached a new low of 41 in July and August 1982. After a plateau, it fell further, to 37 in early January of 1983, to 35 in late January. Only two modern presidents had ever been that low: Richard Nixon, who soon thereafter resigned, and

Jimmy Carter, whose low standing had helped Reagan assist him into early retirement.

Reagan's Democratic critics in the Senate had little reason to be gleeful over his troubles. They, too, were experiencing unkind reactions from the public. Not as severe as the president's and harder to see because the senators were rated by home state publics in polls that were not very frequent or very visible, nonetheless Democratic senators in the aggregate were in decline. Whatever their personal standing in the home state, most in 1982 were lower than they had been before. If they had hoped that Ronald Reagan's troubles would be their good fortune, they would be disappointed. As the economy went from warm to cool to grim, Republican senators, like their party leader in the White House, saw their personal popularity back home decline. But the decline was almost the same for their colleagues across the aisle, the Democrats. Governors of the fifty states were also affected. The national recession meant state tax increases and painful budget cuts, both of which were much in evidence the next fiscal year. For a discontented public there seemed plenty of blame to go around. When asked how someone was doing his or her job, it didn't seem to matter much who that someone was and what in fact he or she had done.

Then, as is usually the case, signs of recovery began to appear even while unemployment was still rising. The last quarter of 1982 saw a return to growth, almost too small to measure. By early 1983 consumer confidence in the economy stopped its year-long decline. Just as Ronald Reagan was reaching bottom, people were, if not confident, at least beginning to doubt their most pessimistic assessments. The first quarter of 1983 produced a full point growth, about a 4 percent annual rate. It could be just an easy adjustment to an economy that had cooled too much or too fast. Or it could be the beginning of recovery.

Reagan approval turned upward, just a little, to about 40, still very low. But consumers and voters saw the turn in the economy this time. The gain in confidence by the second quarter was a real jump. Reagan, who had claimed that what was now called Reaganomics was responsible for the 1981 relatively good showing, had not been eager to attach his name to the recession that followed. By 1983 he was beginning again to claim credit.

By mid-1983 Reagan's approval numbers were in the middle 40s, up about 25 percent from the disastrous 35 of January. Reagan was the enemy of government. "Government isn't the solution," he said over and over again. "Government is the problem." When he had said that in 1982, the public had agreed. Trust in government was near an all-time low. Now in

1983, as Reagan began to recover, the public's esteem for government did, too. And it liked Congress a little better than it had before, and it notched up its approval of U.S. senators, Reagan's friends on the Republican side and his Democratic foes alike. Governors, more victims of economic cycles than its causes, had suffered along with the president, but with a lag. The year 1983 was very bad for them.

The third quarter of 1983 produced a surge of growth. It was so substantial that it could not be anything but recovery. By mid-1983 the economy had made up the ground lost since 1981. By the end of that year it had moved solidly ahead. Then it was no longer in recovery; it was on its way to prosperity. By the last days of 1983 Ronald Reagan moved back into positive territory, reaching an approval of 54 percent. And as he did, Congress looked better, government regained trust, and senators and governors began to breathe easier. The dawn of election year 1984 produced a spirit of optimism. It would carry Reagan to easy victory over Walter Mondale, and times were good, too, for Reagan friends and foes in government, national and state.

Ronald Reagan made the transition from one of the least to one of the most approved presidents. And as he did, citizens began to approve everybody who governed, more than they had before. They began to like Congress better and to trust government more.

What was going on? Why did all those disparate things move together? What does it mean? We have worried about how much people trust government for thirty years or so. We worry because trust is seen as the cement of democracy. It has been lower in recent decades than when first measured. When it is low we ask why and look to alienation of a fundamental sort for explanation. Do people no longer believe in democratic institutions? What has government done to cause distrust? Is it too much scandal, too much regulation? Is it policies that fail, or something more fundamental, such as a loss of belief?

Approval we do not worry about. We think that presidents are approved when they are popular, personable, do popular things, and preside over good times. Declining approval, such as Reagan's in 1982, connotes simply that the public is not happy with outcomes. Its fix isn't a restoration of belief or faith, but simply better outcomes.

There is a vigorous debate among political observers about what role, if any, various parts of government play in regulating the economy. We debate in particular whether presidents are due either credit or blame for prosperity or recession when they are in the White House. Economists least of all believe that presidential policies have major influence for good or ill. The public, in contrast, seems to have no such doubts about efficacy.

It credits presidents specifically for good times and blames them for bad times. Perhaps it is like baseball managers. They neither bat nor field, but are held responsible for their team's fortunes. The president is America's manager.

If presidential responsibility is problematic, what of Congress and its individual members? Congress has a role in taxing and spending and so, hypothetically, can be held responsible for economic outcomes. But it is very hypothetical. We expect economic leadership from the White House. The 535 individual members of House and Senate lack the leverage to lead. They can vote yes or no to proposals, but originating economic regulation is unlikely in our constitutional structure. Nonetheless, good times produce approval of Congress (the institution) and of its individual members.

Governors are not economic policy makers at all, not even hypothetically. They have no say in monetary policy, constitutionally reserved to the federal government, and their mandate to balance state budgets deprives them of any fiscal leverage as well. They respond to the economy but have no control of it.[1] But when the Federal Reserve or the president or the unseen hand – take your choice – moves the economy into prosperity, governors are seen to be "handling their job" as governor. And that approval is withdrawn in bad times.

In this chapter I want to come to terms with what it means for citizens to approve or disapprove individual officeholders and government institutions, to trust or distrust "government" itself. My point of view is that all these things are more interconnected than the words of the questions would suggest and therefore can't mean quite what we think they mean. I begin with the presidency, an office long evaluated and one for which much is known.

THE PRESIDENCY

Presidential approval is part of American culture. Along with the presidential horse race polls, it is grist for conversation by ordinary people. If

---

[1] Governors do work hard at economic development, an action that can pay off in prosperity gains over the long term. But this has little at all to do with the short-term economic cycles that so plague state budget processes. The evidence is that all states tend to experience good and bad times together. They are the tail of the national economy, not the dog. (This was written before the recall of Gray Davis in California, held responsible for a sagging economy and resulting state fiscal shortfalls. California voters, it appears, have expressed the view that the state tail wags the national dog.)

someone on the street is asked what the president's approval rating is, the reading might not be accurate, but the question, also would not draw a dumbfounded stare. It is even evident in Hollywood, where ratings play a starring role in movies such as *The American President* and *Wag the Dog*.

Theories of what affects presidential approval are pretty well known, too. Often seen in political science journals, they are also common fare in news reports and commentaries. The ideas that new presidents have approval honeymoons or that approval surges in response to foreign crises won't be new to many readers of this book. They've worked their way out of regression analyses and into mainstream fare.

Because much is known and because I have been writing about the matter for a quarter of a century (since the Nixon administration), I don't want to belabor presidential approval here.[2] Too important to omit, I restrict myself to laying out a little summary of where we stand and what we know, giving some emphasis to that which is not in movies or daily press reports. I begin with a description of the approval of three recent presidents (leaving out George W. Bush, the very most recent, because the record is too short as I write).

Three Recent Presidents

Presidential approval varies a lot, and that is within administrations, not among them. Although presidents are sometimes characterized as popular or not, the deeper reality is that almost all presidents experience striking variation within their terms. Approval given at one time in the presidency is withdrawn at others.

Ronald Reagan's wild ride was not over with the exuberant 1983–84 recovery. His second term saw his approval plunge again in 1986 over the Iran-Contra scandal (see Fig. 5.1). His vice president, George Bush, set new volatility records. His peak during the Gulf War was the highest ever achieved to that date (now surpassed by his son following the September 11 terrorism).[3] It was followed by a steep plunge into

---

[2] John Mueller's *War, Presidents, and Public Opinion* (1973) is an early source of ideas about what moves presidential approval, a thirty-year-old story that is still basically correct.

[3] A note about the numbers: The approval ratings that appear in Figure 5.1 and others that follow are monthly estimates from the ratings produced by all survey organizations. The act of aggregating over several survey houses and a month or quarter takes out the highest of the highs and the lowest of the lows. Bush provides an example of this effect. In mid-January 1991, following the onset of the decisive ground war, he recorded ratings in the 90s in some polls. The rating of about 85 shown in the figure reflects all polls and it is the whole month, not just the period after the ground war.

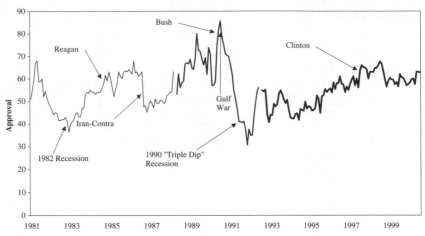

FIGURE 5.1. Gallup approval ratings for three recent presidents, 1981 to 2001.

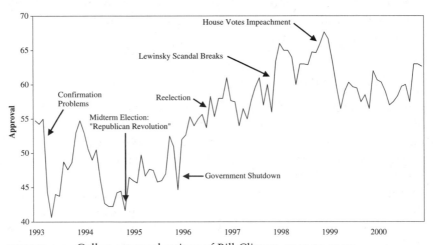

FIGURE 5.2. Gallup approval ratings of Bill Clinton, 1993 to 2001.

percentages in the 30s as a sour economy overwhelmed memory of the war and left him vulnerable to defeat by Bill Clinton. Bill Clinton's ratings are the least volatile of the three. His lows were not as low as Reagan or Bush and his highs were not as high. What is remarkable in Clinton's public standing is that it increased while he weathered the storm of the Lewinsky scandal.

I examine the Clinton presidency in more detail in Figure 5.2. Bill Clinton took office with relatively low approval. Like Reagan and Bush before him (and the other Bush to come), Clinton did not have the traditional beginning-of-term honeymoon. That tradition is clearly no longer traditional. Clinton's early months in office were rocky. His early reputation was as a politician who would yield when he encountered resistance. And he encountered a lot of it as he tried to put his administration in place, much of it from his own party in Congress.

With signs of progress in the economy, Clinton's standing with the public recovered from some early losses, setting the stage for his priority health care proposal in Congress. The loss of that proposal put Clinton in trouble again in 1994. More than the typical legislative fight, this one affected the reputation of the president. Republicans in Congress, led by Newt Gingrich, energized by defeating Clinton on health care, approached the 1994 midterm elections with their "Contract with America" and with unusual confidence. The election turned out to be a bigger Clinton defeat than health care had been, a forty-year turning point in party control of the House of Representatives. Widely seen as a rejection of the Clinton presidency – a view Clinton himself did not dispute – it would be his low point.

Republicans in Congress took over governing. Ignoring the president's proposals, they set out first passing the elements of the "contract" and then began a year-long struggle to control the budget. Beginning in the spring of 1995, Gingrich announced that Republicans would pass the kind of budget they wanted, ignoring the "irrelevant" Clinton, and laid out a strategy that entailed shutting down the government at the end of the fiscal year if Clinton did not sign their appropriations bills. When the shutdown came, it was more disruptive and painful than most expected. The Republican gamble on the struggle with Clinton did not work. Since the strategy of the shutdown was advertised in advance, the public mainly took Clinton's side against Congress, seeing Congress, not the president, as the obstructionist element. It was a defining moment for Clinton, the first of many in which his Republican opponents unintentionally aided the president's public standing. From that moment the previously unpopular Clinton had a three-year run of ever-growing approval, with an ever-growing economy contributing much to his standing.

That Clinton run included a huge *increase* in approval following revelation of the Lewinsky scandal. What are we to make of that? A straightforward reading of the data – that the public liked Clinton better with scandal than without – will not satisfy many. What then accounts for the increase? The theory of considerations is helpful here. If we ask what people were talking about following the revelation, and therefore which issue was fresh in their minds, it was, "Should he stay or should he go?" Imagine in that context that you are asked the "handling his job" question, and it is likely that you will see it as an opportunity to vote on the stay-or-go question. So the greater approval probably reflects a shift of frame from "Do I approve?" to "Should he stay in office?" Some who wouldn't have been moved to approval nonetheless do not want the constitutional crisis of a president turned out of office by an opposition Congress.

A similar, but smaller jump occurred after the December 1998 House vote to impeach Clinton. The same explanation seems right. What of the true effect of the Lewinsky scandal? That is seen, I think, in the falloff of Clinton approval after the impeachment crisis was over. That falloff is not huge, but it occurs for a president presiding over peace and an eight-year run of prosperity unmatched in modern times.

Some Basic Facts and Theories

If we look further, to the presidencies of the survey era, we can see that general patterns do emerge in most administrations and do not require a focus on particular events. I turn now to that more general accounting.

Equilibration

Underlying all the things that cause approval to be up sometimes and down at others, what operates in the background is equilibration. It is the sort of "dark matter" in our theory, the unseen force that counterbalances that which we observe. The story is a simple one: When presidents are for some reason too high or too low in approval, and nothing happens but the passage of time, they tend to move back toward an equilibrium. Whatever it was that caused them to be too high or too low, that is, decays as time passes. This is important in a statistical sense, but also in politics. There is much speculation about the things presidents might do to draw attention and gain a few points in the polls. The theme of the movie *Wag the Dog*, but also a lot of serious writing about politics, it seems that presidents need only create some drama and they can repair damage to their standing whenever it is needed. From the president's point of view that seems too good to be true, and it is. What those accounts fail to factor in is that approval gains can decay just about as fast as they are created. And anything that depends on drama and novelty won't last. A president who perennially created drama to boost approval would be on a treadmill, always having to restore by new activity that which is constantly eroding.

Of the equilibrium we know two things. One is that it is close to 50 percent approval. Presidents above that in the polls tend to decline back toward it. Those below it tend to recover upward to it. That seems a sort of magic number, but this is probably coincidence.[4] The second is that there is a lot less variation between presidents on this matter than press reports would imply. Although there are observable differences, they are small. It is not the case that we can label some of them popular and others unpopular and still do justice to the data.

Crises

Crises are the opposite force, dramatic events capable of moving approval away from – sometimes a long way from – equilibrium approval. In situations in which the nation is in peril against external threats, particularly, Americans "rally around the flag" (Mueller 1973), coming to the support of the president, standing as the national symbol. It is hard to imagine that it could be otherwise. Normally the spokesperson for a political party allied against another party and half of the electorate that supports it, presidents can hardly expect approval to move far into the other side. Moments of crisis change that. Then there are no parties and no opposition, but only a single nation with a single leader. When the president acts for all, he or she can begin to expect approval for that action from all. It is very different from the "us and them" of normal politics.

Normalcy will always prevail in the long run. Thus the approval gained from crisis can never be expected to last. We are tempted always to regard each new crisis as different, *this time* redefining the nature of the polity. But the immediacy of crisis, the drama, is precisely what guarantees that it will not last. Crises get resolved, one way or another, and then they cease to be crises, cease to be dramatic, cease to have any effect on the president's public standing. Crises are punctuations, moments when the relentless return to equilibrium is halted. But the return will always take over.

We don't know about the really long term. Presidencies don't last long enough to know. Most episodes leave no further trace in the approval standings after about a year or so; smaller and sharper episodes can disappear more quickly. While there is often speculation that such temporary

---

[4] Since the convention in approval studies is to use the simple percentage who say "approve" – and there is always some small percent who will not supply an answer – an approval rating of 50 means than more than half of those expressing an opinion approve. It is not a neutral point. An exact 49.8 is estimated in Erikson et al. 2002.

surges might be enough to carry a president through a reelection, there is no clear case where that has been so. Jimmy Carter's approval boosting crisis was the Iranian hostage situation. A year later the boost was all gone and the unresolved situation became a drag on Carter's standing. George Bush benefited from the Gulf War crisis as had no president before him. But like Carter, Bush's benefit deserted him before voters went to the polls.[5]

The Honeymoon

The presidential honeymoon, a time of hope and expectation (with no tangible basis for disapproval), was a nice tradition. A kind of laying on of the hands of democracy, there was a nice symbolism to it. The people had spoken. The nation was one. The winner had a righteous claim to lead. It is easier to understand why it existed than why it appears to have gone. Millions of people, relatively independent of party, relatively neutral and moderate of viewpoint, have naturally adopted new presidents. They have acted as if public support was a right won by election, the president's to own until he did something to lose it. Brody (1991) points to a critical role for the media and the opposition party in this phenomenon. So long as the opposition does not criticize the new president, he writes, the media will not do so, either. Mostly commercial, media outlets need to minimize offending their listeners and subscribers if they are to be financially successful. And independent media attacks on the president, particularly a newly elected one, are potentially offensive. The constraint within which the media operate is that the parties effectively define the boundaries of what is legitimate and what is not. The space between them, between support and opposition, is legitimate ground for media commentary. Outside them, particularly being more critical than the opposition, is dangerous – and so editors and reporters do not go there. That effectively relegates the control of presidential criticism to the opposition; if it holds its fire, everybody holds back. If it attacks the president, then it can expect that the media will also engage in a less partisan form of presidential criticism. Brody's thesis then predicts the honeymoon as a natural consequence of

---

[5] It can be argued that the Gulf War may even have played a role in Bush's defeat. While Bush was basking in remarkable public adulation, the American economy was in the tank. Had there been no war and no popularity surge, it seems likely that Bush would have gotten ahead of the political curve of recession, at least to the limited degree possible. As it was, the Bush White House miscalculated that the war-induced approval was bankable political capital that would allow Bush his preferred, hands-off stance on the economy.

a long tradition of withholding partisan criticism of presidents in their earliest months.

As American politics has become more polarized and conflictual, that tradition has disappeared. Party leaders on both sides now see it as their duty to rough up a new president of the other party lest he become too popular. Since the presidential honeymoon is as impermanent as the new marriage phenomenon for which it is named, I do not understand quite why this is the case. It would seem that the honeymoon would always fall of its own weight eventually in any case. When the president is no longer new, the factors that produced it lose force.

Perhaps we are dealing with exceptions here, that it is something about these particular presidents and these particular years that suppressed the tendency to honor the honeymoon. But Presidents Reagan, Bush, Clinton, and now George W. Bush constitute four exceptions in a row, spanning twenty years. That's a pretty big exception.

The National Economy

However much or little presidents have to do with regulating the economy, the economy definitely does regulate them. Movements in economic outcomes translate pretty directly into approval and disapproval. Not as dramatic as crises, economic effects are probably more important because they can be enduring. The approval gain from a recovery, for example, can grow strongly and steadily over time, changing the character of a presidency.

It is natural to see reaction to the economy as reward and punishment, tied to individual self-interest. In this "pocketbook" view, individuals approve when they and their families are prospering and take out anger for personal misfortune on the president. Although some such individual effects can be teased out of very complicated statistical analyses, most of the observable connection between economics and political response is what Kinder and Kiewiet (1979) call "sociotropic," evaluations based on the state of the national economy, not the personal pocketbook. This can be understood as resulting from the ease or difficulty of causal attribution. The connection between presidential action and individual economic situations is so distant that it is virtually impossible to assess it. (People do connect them, often with a partisan bias, but this isn't economic evaluation, but rather a rationalization for a view held for other reasons.) It is easier to hold the president responsible for the contours of the national economy, how things are going in general.

Another traditional view, that people first *experience* the economy and then evaluate the president, also does not hold. What the data say, in contrast, is that people evaluate the president on how they *expect* the economy to be months and years down the road (MacKuen, Erikson, and Stimson 1992). Optimism and pessimism are crucial ingredients of the political translation of economic views. When things are bad, but expected to get better, presidents do well. When they are good, but the public sees indicators of decline, approval will fall. This can be seen as a minor wrinkle in the economic picture. But it has a major consequence. It implies that governments cannot manufacture approval by trickery, by measures that might induce temporary surges of prosperity timed, for example, for elections. A public focused on the future does not fall for these tricks.

The view of presidential control we end with is in some sense hopeful. Presidents do affect their fates by achieving, or failing to achieve, the peace and prosperity the public desires. But when so much of politics is manipulation and spin, it appears to be the case that approval cannot be manufactured by the most sophisticated political trickery, cannot be bought by public relations.[6] Modern presidents jawbone the economy from time to time, telling citizens that things are good, that presidential policies are due credit. The public, it appears, mimics the financial markets in this regard and makes up its own mind.

U.S. SENATORS

On thousands of occasions, surveys have asked respondents to evaluate one or both of their U.S. senators. It is not clear what ought to underlie such evaluations or what does. Mostly, the evaluations are assumed to tap individual skill at pleasing constituents and they are assumed to impinge on senators' reelection prospects. The purpose is to gauge state public opinion, usually on the assumption that state publics differ a good deal from one another.[7]

---

[6] This generalization is on firm ground for matters domestic, where it appears that the public always knows enough to judge for itself. Beyond the borders, the president's information advantage grows and so possibly does the prospect of successful deception.

[7] Data on senator and governor approval ratings are from the Job Approval Ratings Database, a cooperative project of the University of Rochester, the University of North Carolina at Chapel Hill, and George Washington University (http://www.unc.edu/~beyle/jars.html).

Building on the work of Anderson and Newmark (2002), I wish here to stand back from all those individual states and ask whether we can learn something about the nation from watching how fifty individual states respond to their senators. If you think about how Senator X is handling his or her job as senator, it is far from clear what standard one should invoke. Senators go to Washington, make speeches, sponsor legislation, vote on bills. For an objective observer, it would seem quite difficult to know whether the senator is "handling" all those things well or badly. One can employ a partisan or ideological standard for what is a good or bad voting record, but the best that you can summon for a neutral standard is whether or not the senator shows up for the votes.

In the absence of useful information for evaluating the senator's performance, we might expect more generic considerations to become important. Party is one of these. Respondents will usually know whether the senator is from their own party or an opponent, from the president's party or an opponent, and whether the two senators are on the same side of the party division. From this we might expect to see differential response to the parties. The action in Washington is often between presidents and the opposing party in Congress. From this we might expect tension between the president's standing and that of the opposition in Congress. When one is up, the other would be down, their two tracks over time negatively correlated.

The same absence of useful individual information might make respondents use general information, such as how things are going in the country, to evaluate their individual senators. We can't observe that senators have anything to do with, for example, the ebbs and flows of the national economy, but lacking any better standard, respondents might just credit everybody for good times and blame everybody for bad ones. Since this same process applies to the White House, we would expect positive correlations between the president's approval and that of all senators.

Thus our two expectations are in conflict. The negative evidence of expecting a see-saw between president and out party would conflict with the positive evidence of a world in which credit and blame go to all. Since it can't be both, a first step is to observe that correlation, to see how the standings of Democrats and Republicans move over time and to see whether they move together or opposite one another.

To do so I take all the approval readings for each party and solve for the average response that underlies them. The result, what Anderson and Newmark call "Senator Approval," is a national summary measure of the disparate responses of the state publics. What is unusual about the

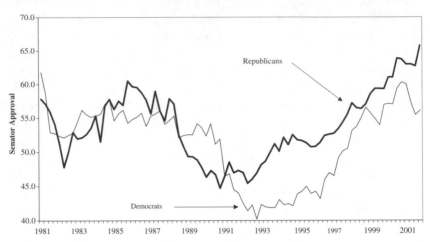

FIGURE 5.3. Senator approval by party, 1981 to 2001.

measure is that it taps response to an institution, the Senate, but by means of responses to individual senators. All the things that individual senators might do becomes a kind of noise around a signal, which is the summary response to the whole Senate (or here to the parties in the Senate.)

The evidence of Figure 5.3 settles the issue. The standing of senators from the two parties tracks together, not opposite. And the "why" is not a mystery. One can clearly see the national economy in the background: a dip around the 1982 recession, a rise in the better times of 1984–89, down again with the 1990–92 triple dip, and a long upward movement with the economy through 2001. And all these things move both parties together. The correlation between the two series is a very high .67. Since the Senate parties are positively correlated and both move with the economic source of presidential approval, then both parties must also be positively correlated with presidential approval, support and opposition alike.

That the general state of things underlies senator approval is no shock. What is more surprising is how little the partisan game in Washington seems to matter. The president and opponents in Congress do battle, acting as if winning and losing really mattered in the ups and downs of the two parties. (And it does really matter for its policy consequences.) But all the posturing seems lost on the electorate, which sees the parties doing well or badly *together*. There is a cynical view around that many legislative contests are just empty debates, votes staged to win or to lose voters in the next election, not to decide policy. If that is true, then these data begin to suggest that it is a wasted effort, that voters don't much care who wins or loses, but just how things are going.

CONGRESS

In a totally different approach – national, not state, and institutional, not individual – respondents are asked what they think of Congress. Because it is the institution, "Congress," and not its individual members, it is less clear what we should expect. And it is a little unclear what this "Congress" is. Is it the House of Representatives, both bodies, some legislative abstraction? We begin with the expectation that Congress will be unpopular on average. A favorite whipping boy of all, including its own members, Congress takes a battering in public discourse. It has many critics and no friends. We thus expect it to be perennially unpopular.

Individual members, such as the U.S. senators we have already seen, have a more favorable situation. Much of what citizens know of them comes from their own activities, which are planned always to cast the member in a favorable light. Members are rarely criticized, except for two or three months before elections, and voters discount that for what it is. But the question we wish to pose for both is, "How do they move?"

Figure 5.4 provides a one-word answer to that question: "together." Whatever gulf divides "Congress" from the hundreds of members who

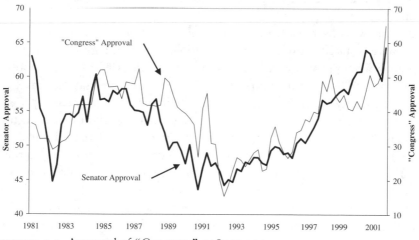

FIGURE 5.4. Approval of "Congress," 1981 to 2001.

serve on its Senate side, the movement over time is two versions of the same story. The movements, correlated at .74, march to the same drummer. But the graphic device of scaling on two axes hides two important differences. Individual senators are much more approved on average (53%) than is Congress (38%). And the reaction to Congress, the institution, is much more varied, its lows dramatically lower than the senators and its highs about the same. Without a lot of confidence in the call, I suggest that the difference arises from a difference of knowledge. Voters really do know something about their senators. They have probably consciously decided to vote for or against them, for example. "Congress" is, in contrast, ephemeral, an image much more than a reality. Because that image is not rooted in much factual exposure, it is free to move with the times, free to change. The evidence that the image can change dramatically, as it did following the September 11 terrorism, for example, suggests that the perennial bad esteem for Congress is not deeply felt, just a casual prejudice, subject to change with each new piece of information.

GOVERNORS

People have direct experience with state governors. Governors are responsible for things close to home, such as schools, highways, and state and local taxation. For most citizens most of the time, this is more immediate than the influence of the federal government. From this we might infer that response to the governors is based on personal experience. If so, it would reflect the particular successes and failures of each state, the idiosyncrasies of state politics.

When we observe a net measure of the governors' standing, however, we see a restatement of the familiar national pattern. Figure 5.5 displays the average approval of governors by state samples with the previously estimated U.S. senator approval for reference. It bears saying that this result is partly inevitable, that a method that solves for average approval across states will discard much of the idiosyncratic variation. That is the intent. But the solution is very highly correlated with each of the individual governor's approval ratings, a fact that is inconsistent with the idea that state publics are different from one another, evaluating their governments on their own issues and politics. The governors, instead, rise and fall in unison with the factors that move response to national politics. All politics is not national, to paraphrase Tip O'Neill. But it is most definitely not local.

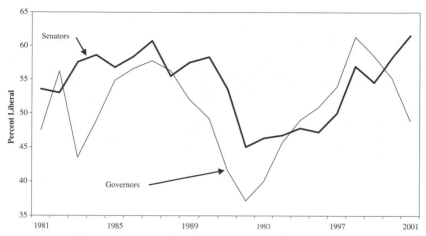

FIGURE 5.5. Governor approval and senator approval, 1981 to 2001.

TRUST IN GOVERNMENT

Trust in government, as noted in the introduction to this chapter, is widely seen to be fundamental. When it declines, it is regarded as pathological, not mere movement. Whether the explanation is declining trust in people on the whole, generalized to government (Easton 1965; Putnam 1995, 2000), or declining trust produced by some kind of alienation and disaffection with government and its acts, decline is worrisome.

An alternative view, developed by Keele (2002, 2003), holds that trust simply follows recent performance. Citizens trust government when it has performed well and withdraw trust when they are displeased with the state of things. As is usually the case, the national economy is the best indicator of performance. Keele shows that trust follows economic indicators and citizen responses such as presidential approval, which themselves are moved by economic outcomes. Trust, in this story, loses its status as barometer of democracy and becomes part of a syndrome of citizen response to everything. It goes up as well as down, and its movements require explanation but not concern.

Figure 5.6, showing trust in government along with the congressional approval series of the earlier Figure 5.4, shows that the Keele view squares nicely with the data. The two different measures, derived from altogether different sources and measuring, in concept, quite different things, track closely together. This, of course, is a pattern now repeated several times. It suggests that something more general than each of these indicators lies beneath, a topic to which I now turn.

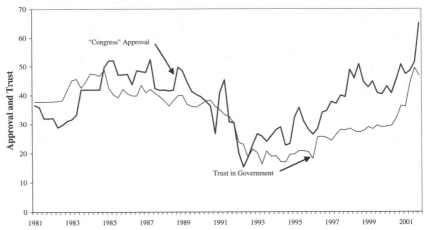

FIGURE 5.6. Trust in government compared with approval of Congress, 1981 to 2001.

IS APPROVAL GENERIC?

It is by now obvious that we are dealing here with something different from what the survey questions seem to mean. When we ask how governors or senators or presidents are handling their jobs, we think the answers reflect on the individuals and institutions that are the focus of the questions. If President Bush is up or down a point or two, we ask what he has done recently and why the public is responding to him as it is. But now we see that it may not be responding to him at all. It may be expressing a generic satisfaction or dissatisfaction with government, for which he is merely beneficiary or victim.[8]

What we are observing is generic approval and trust, a spirit that moves up and down over time and seems to respond to generalized satisfaction or dissatisfaction with the state of things. To express the idea, imagine that we can simply take all the approval and trust series, forget *whose* approval is being queried, and just estimate a generic approval over time.[9] Figure 5.7 captures that generic approval for the twenty-one-year span where we have numerous measures of each. The figure, showing the

---

[8] This view borrows elements from Rahn (2000) in which the concept of "mood" (very different from my "policy mood" of Chapter 3) ties together disparate reactions to political life.

[9] I don't quite forget the "who"; the technique averages over a time series of each of the objects of evaluation.

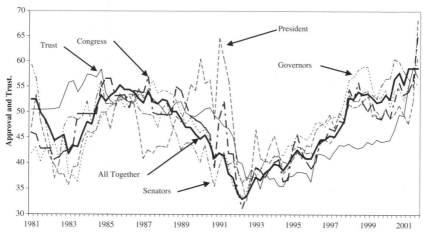

FIGURE 5.7. Generic approval, with approval of presidents, senators, governors, Congress, and trust in government.

estimate of generic approval along with each of its components (standardized to squeeze them together in the space), shows the now familiar shape: declines in 1982, upturns in the mid-1980s, serious decline in 1990–92, followed by steady increases over the 1990s.

We can see some differences among the individual series. Presidential approval stands out from the others in 1986–87, when the Iran-Contra scandal lowered Ronald Reagan's standing but didn't affect that of others. And then George Bush stood out first in 1989, for a honeymoon not observable except in contrast to other trends, and then dramatically in 1991 at the time of the Gulf War. The low point of approval of Congress, just barely discernible, comes in 1992 with the House Banking Scandal. And the 1998–99 Lewinsky scandal period is interesting. We know that the scandal appeared to help Bill Clinton, so we would not expect to find much influence. But what is noticeable is a decline of trust in government during the scandal, accompanied by governors moving above the national government figures. The common pattern that would make sense of these movements is a joint disapproval of both Clinton and his opponents in Congress during the conflict.

The most important point, however, is that the lines are hard to pull apart and distinguish because they are pretty clearly measuring the same thing. Mainly what we see in Figure 5.7 is mostly random variation around a common movement that applies to all these presumably different series. Approval and trust are generic, a syndrome of attitudes toward public

FIGURE 5.8. Generic approval and the Michigan Index of Consumer Sentiment (three-quarter moving average).

affairs that only appears to be affected by and directed toward particular people and institutions.

A description of shared movements of Figure 5.7 will sound to readers a lot like a description of the U.S. economy: 1982 recession, followed by 1983–89 recovery, followed by the 1990 recession – becoming the triple dip downturn over 1990–92, followed by the steadily improving prosperity of the 1990s. It is evident that all those approval and trust measures tap some satisfaction and dissatisfaction with outcomes.

We can see more than a suggestion of that fact in Figure 5.8, which graphs the generic approval series against the University of Michigan consumer sentiment index, a generalized measure of citizen views of the economy. The two series have different measurement scales, with consumer sentiment normed around a neutral point of 100 (although the actual long-term average is considerably under 100). Thus, they are presented with separate scales on two axes. The pattern, however, is robust. Satisfied consumers are approving citizens. The two track quite closely together, with consumer sentiment leading approval by a quarter or two, sentiment tracking sharply with the twists and turns of the economy, while approval follows later.

Again, we can make some sense of discrepancies between the two. The 1991 Gulf War helped approval to stay high when confidence in the economy was falling. Perhaps it is mere accident or measurement issue, but it seems telling that economic confidence was consistently stronger during the Clinton presidency than was approval of all sorts. What we know about these years is that they mark intense partisan conflict, particularly 1994–2000, with the government shutdown in 1995–96 quickly followed by the Lewinsky scandal becoming an impeachment crisis in 1998–99. Conflict is unappealing to the public, likely to hurt the standing of all parties to it. So, for example, even if Bill Clinton may have been the *net* winner in the contest with the Republican Congress over the government shutdown (in my earlier interpretation), these data are consistent with an interpretation that conflict drags down public approval of government in general. (And we know from the previous figure that the state governors, not involved in that mess in Washington, became more approved than their national counterparts in this period.)

Generic approval and economic confidence are not identical, to be sure. Note the divergence following the September 11, 2001, terrorism. As approval for all aspects of government soared, confidence in the economy tanked at the same time. We also can be reasonably sure that the economy is not the whole story. While nothing else is apparent for this limited twenty-one-year period, we know that events such as the Vietnam War and the Watergate scandal had huge impacts on presidential approval, and that presidential approval tracks with the others. Thus, if these events were captured in our data, we would expect to see systematic influence.

So what does it mean that citizens approve or trust? It appears to mean mainly that things are going well in the country. What is important about this pattern, and unexpected, is that the approval and trust are granted to those who have had no role in producing the outcomes. We have known for some time that presidents seemed to get more credit or blame than they deserved. With the pattern now extended to those who have had no conceivable role, we need to reassess what it means to approve.

We need not reassess the consequences of approval. They are repeatedly demonstrated and very large. Baseball managers do get fired and disapproved politicians do lose elections. It's just where that approval or disapproval came from that can be puzzling.

6

On Politics at the Margin

Everywhere we have looked we have seen order. We have seen a public opinion that responds smoothly and predictably to public events. And what is predictable also is appropriate. Notwithstanding powerful evidence of individual ignorance and inattention, collective public opinion is everywhere orderly. We saw it in opinion response to events in Chapter 2, in alignments with parties over time in Chapter 3, in the daily fluctuations of the horse race polls in Chapter 4, and in response to government and politicians in Chapter 5. Everywhere order.

And yet we know that most Americans know and care little about government. I believe in that evidence of ignorance and inattention and have gathered some of it myself. How can we square the massive evidence of ignorance and unconcern about politics in the American public with the order we have repeatedly seen in the last five chapters?

The evidence is, after all, real. Most Americans do not know much about public affairs and report – with no apparent embarrassment – that they also don't care a great deal. And the evidence of the orderly aggregate is real. How, then, can we make sense of the two jointly? How do we get out of this dilemma?

The beginning point is understanding that politics happens at the margin. Political change occurs when a percent or two of the public changes opinions or changes sides. That's all it takes. The mass can remain a combination of the committed and the inert, neither of which moves in response to much of anything, while just a very few are sensitive to the changing signals of governance.

Great movements to left or right, to Democrat or Republican, or to approval or disapproval are produced by the systematic change of a quite small number of people. Our politics have not the flavor of the evangelist's tent, where great numbers repent their past and change. We do not throw off commitments to party or ideology lightly or en masse. Instead, what counts as political change, even dramatic political change, is produced by quite small numbers of people moving systematically.

Note some parallelism to the aggregation gain argument of Chapter 1. Aggregation gain is a principle of mathematics; it has nothing to do with politics. This is now a more substantive point about politics, that the range of possibilities is mainly small-scale shifts around the middle. In other aspects of life, one can imagine large-scale changes back and forth over time. In American politics, outcomes are held near the middle. Our winner-take-all structure of power makes it seem that our politics veer back and forth on wild swings. And that is true of the consequences of party control. The party that has 50 percent plus one seat in the House of Representatives, for example, wins everything. Thus we experience sharp alterations between liberalism and conservatism. But the numbers that underlie control shift very little at all.

How is politics different? One reason, taken up below, is that most Americans contribute nothing to movement over time. Some are committed to a position for a lifetime and have no reason ever to change. Others are so uninvolved that their movements lack pattern, canceling out in the aggregate. Only a relatively small number are free to move and pay enough attention to move systematically.

Here I take up the scale of political change in America, asking how much movement it takes to move American politics.

A TALE OF THREE ELECTIONS

In an equally divided nation, in theory, a single voter – say, number 50,000,001 out of 100,000,001, the median on a left-right scale – controls election outcomes. And setting aside issues of spoiled ballots and the like, that mathematical abstraction was fairly descriptive of the Florida vote that elected George W. Bush in 2000.

We don't, of course, expect a single voter ever to produce an election result. But the point is that it is possible. The related point, closer to electoral reality, is that when elections tend to divide very close to the 50–50 line, then the systematic choices of a very small proportion of the electorate, 1 or 2 percent, can be decisive.

How close is close? Consider the three most recent elections to the House of Representatives. They form a handy benchmark. The first of

them, in 1998, is considered a Democratic win. The Democrats picked up
five House seats, an impressive achievement against the pattern, unbroken
since 1934, that the party of the White House always loses seats in midterm
elections. That was followed by a near standoff, a two-seat Republican
pickup, in the razor-thin presidential race of 2000. And then in 2002 the
party of George W. Bush also beat the historical odds and gained five
House seats.

Now we can ask, how much does it take to turn a Democratic win
(1998) into a Republican win (2002)? How many voters have to change
sides to produce this outcome? Using the 2002 two-party vote – a little
over 70 million – as a total turnout estimate for both contests, we can
calculate the exact number of voters who would need to change sides in
order to produce the observed totals for the two elections. That number,
about 1,275,000, is twice the number who would need to switch from
Democrat to Republican between 1998 and 2002. Thus, 637,500 voters
(a little fewer than the population of Memphis, Tennessee) could have
altered who was celebrating and who was vowing to do better on the two
election nights.[1]

These are close elections, perhaps the easiest case to show that small
numbers can produce big results. Consider the hardest case: How many
voters have to shift to account for the difference between the best Democratic showing in recent decades (the post-Watergate 1974 election, with
58.7% of the two-party vote) and the worst, the 1994 "Republican Revolution" (46.4%)? The answer (again using the 2002 turnout totals for
simplicity) is about 8.6 million – a result that could have been produced
if all residents of Los Angeles switched from Democratic (1974) to Republican (1994) and everyone else stood pat. And that number is as big
as it gets.

Figure 6.1 shows the House election outcomes series for all elections
of the last half-century. Its vertical axis, covering only the twenty-point
range from 40 to 60 percent Democratic shares, tells part of the story.
The other 80 percent of possible outcomes isn't needed.[2] What one can
see is very little back and forth, but rather two eras, before 1994, where
the Democrats averaged a little under 54 percent, and 1994 and after,
where they are reduced to a little under 49 percent on average.

---

[1] This calculation assumes constant turnout. If we let the base for the calculation be the
roughly 200 million Americans who *might* have voted, then the 0.9 point shift becomes
less than 0.3 percent of eligible Americans.
[2] A graph using the full 0–100 range is so undifferentiated that it looks like a picket fence
done with some lack of skill.

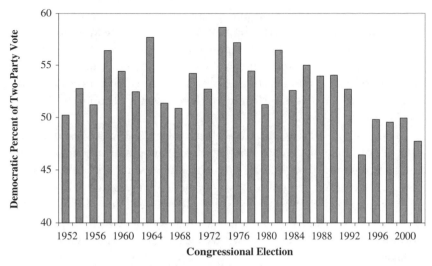

FIGURE 6.1. Democratic votes shares in house elections, 1952–2002.

Explaining these outcomes doesn't require many switches of votes. Because some offset others, we don't know how many voters changed in these elections. But the systematic changers, those moving toward the winning party, constitute less than a percent of the electorate in the 1998–2002 illustration and about 6 percent at the outer-limit 1974–94 comparison. If the game of politics were played on a football field, the goalposts would be erected at the forty-five-yard lines, not in the end zones, and points would be awarded for crossing midfield. Political change that matters is at the margin.

To understand how so few can account for large shifts in outcomes, we need to come to terms with the sorts of people who are and are not available for conversion.

We are all surrounded by like-minded people to some degree. And thus we share a common bias in believing that others are more like us than they really are. This is particularly true in politics, where all of those who act on the stage or who tell us what the play means, and virtually all of those emotionally involved in the drama, come from the same small class of politically involved and literate people, who are very much unlike typical Americans. To be a professional student of public opinion is to engage in many casual conversations, the cocktail party sort, and be told on some point, "Everybody I know feels this way," expressing the "consensus" point of view of 1 or 2 percent.

Strong views on one side are offset by equally strong views on the other. But what both sides fail to see is how atypical it is to hold strong views on either side. Passionate liberals and conservatives agree with one another on the meaning of their struggle, neither realizing that most Americans don't see it that way at all. The random selection procedures of survey research get us beyond the limits of who we happen to know and open a vista of styles of thinking about politics that are quite rare inside the Beltway where politics is performed or in the editorial room, where conflict is explained.

Most people, it turns out, don't think like those who dominate our view of politics: politicians, journalists, academics (and anyone whose interest in politics is so atypically high that they would willingly read this book!). They don't see politics as a struggle of ideas and world-views, don't emotionally commit to one side, and neither know nor care about the issue debates that so move the actors on the stage. That's pretty important, because without them we would not have meaningful political change.

WHO ACCOUNTS FOR CHANGE IN AMERICAN POLITICS?

When the public changes, who changes? The question, like "Who is buried in Grant's tomb?," seems to answer itself. The answer seems obvious. But it isn't. Change at the margin of 1 or 2 or 3 percent, enough to dramatically shift political outcomes, can be the product – in theory – of 1 or 2 or 3 percent of the electorate. If they moved with perfect uniformity, say, two out of every 100 Americans could account for a visible impetus for change or the difference between Democratic and Republican wins at the polls. While 98 percent stood still, 2 percent could move and produce a 2 percent change.

The point here is that we don't need 50 or 80 or 100 percent of all citizens to respond to some signal in order to observe meaningful net change. And while we probably need more than 2 percent for a net 2 percent change, we don't need a lot more than that.[3]

More than just numbers accounts for change. We know something about who is likely to change political views. Imagine that we can classify all citizens into one of three simple categories.[4]

---

[3] Unidirectional moves do occur. In the face of gloomy news about the national economy, for example, some people will move to disapproval of the president, and they will not be offset by a countermovement toward approval.

[4] This treatment borrows from a similar logic, applied only to partisanship, in Erikson et al. 2002.

The Passionate

There are, first, the passionate people who care a great deal about public affairs, have strong views, and form lasting commitments to one side or the other. The ranks of the passionate include the best informed and most politically involved Americans (and most of those reading this book). While it is possible to be informed about and involved in politics while remaining neutral, few choose to do so. Those who care generally take sides. Those who care passionately generally make lifetime commitments. The defining characteristic of the passionate, then, is commitment. If politics is a cause and politicians are chosen for where they stand, then change is never necessary. The committed ideologue can – and should – be constant over a lifetime.

Readers will find the cognitive style of the passionate familiar. It is the style of most of those observed in politics and equally most of those doing the observing. They are nonetheless a small proportion of Americans.

The Scorekeepers

A second group, the scorekeepers, lacks the commitment of the passionate.[5] The scorekeepers are nonideological pragmatists who trust or distrust each side equally. They tend to see politics not as a contest of worldviews, but merely as alternate teams of possible managers of government, each contending that they can do a better job. The scorekeepers are not choosing directions in their votes; they are hiring managers. Where the passionate ask of politicians, "Are their views correct?," the scorekeepers ask, "Will they do a good job?"

The Uninvolved

The final group, everybody else, lacks the interest and involvement of the others, and mostly doesn't pay attention. People who think politics isn't important in their lives (and they probably are right), don't pay

---

[5] My view is very much influenced here by the "running tally" notions of partisanship developed in Fiorina (1981). The style of the argument differs in that Fiorina proposed the running tally as a cognitive device for all citizens (and only for partisanship), whereas I locate a particular group of people who think about politics this way and generalize it to all aspects of opinion. The substance, nonetheless, is still very much the Fiorina idea.

attention and don't want to be bothered.[6] Because they are inattentive, their views are not responsive to the happenings of politics. Failing to observe the stimulus, they do not produce the response. The movements of the uninvolved have a random character. Moved by something, they are not moved by the systematic information flow seen by their attentive counterparts.

With a lot of work we could put numbers on the three. But the categories are probably not constant over time anyhow, and so I won't bother. Whatever the true sizes, one-third, one-third, and one-third is a decent approximation. We now know enough to answer the question of who produces movement. The answer is that the middle group, the scorekeepers, accounts for virtually all change over time. While a first intuition might be that the passionate must be important movers, *not moving* is their defining characteristic. They never switch sides. Like players in a football match, they never take off their jerseys and sit themselves on the opposite bench. So when politics changes, they cannot be the agents of change.

The uninvolved also produce no aggregate change. Not attentive to the signals that move other citizens, they move, but not in concert. Random individual movements are self-canceling in the aggregate.

Now, to explain change at the margin we now know that we are dealing with the behaviors of only a part of the electorate, a key part that has two attributes: (1) paying enough attention to respond to the common signals of politics, yet (2) not being so involved as to be committed always to one side. They then produce all of our evidence of systematic change.

So if we ask what is typical of American politics in the aggregate, we are really asking what moves the scorekeepers. Immediately, it becomes clear that all of the evidence of "typical" citizens is irrelevant to explaining change over time. The citizen attributes that matter are those of the scorekeepers alone.

And that matters. When we believed falsely that what was typical of individual citizens would be typical of the nation, it was devastating to learn, for example, that 20 percent or so did not know which party controlled Congress, which was due credit or blame for its acts. But if all 20 percent come from the ranks of the uninvolved, then that terrible

---

[6] It would be wrong, however, to assert that a large group of Americans *never* pays attention. Some breakthrough events, such as sex in the White House or the September 11 terrorism, command the attention of virtually all.

lapse of political knowledge has no consequence for the *electorate's* ability to reward or punish.

Political economy provides another example. We have similarly known for some time that the passionate filter their perceptions of the national economy through a partisan screen. Opponents of the president underestimate the economy's real strength and proponents overestimate it. This effect is very large. And the uninvolved often seem to be talking about *another* economy, so loose is their grasp of the simple facts of employment and inflation. But none of these lapses is consequential. The net perception of the economy, neither biased nor ignorant, is driven wholly by the scorekeepers. It is right on the mark. (Erikson et al. 2002)

THE RHYTHMS OF OPINION: A RECONSIDERATION

We now have two ideas: Important political change occurs at the margin, and the citizens who produce it are a rare substratum of those who are dispassionate and still reasonably well informed. My goal in the rest of this chapter is to use those twin ideas to explain some of the patterns of earlier chapters. I wish to make sense of strong claims about how much the electorate knows and how it acts in the face of massive evidence of ignorance and inattention.

On Policy Preferences

Across most issues public views move in parallel. Liberalism and conservatism in public preferences rise and fall in concert, the public changing its attitude toward government action in environment, welfare, urban aid, race, education, defense spending, and other issues all at the same time. This common national mood we know responds thermostatically to government policy. Mood becomes more conservative under liberal governments, more liberal under conservative regimes.

That requires some attentiveness. It requires citizens in the aggregate to know who is governing – and recall that many citizens fail the simple test of knowledge of which party controls Congress – and more than that, to know the direction of policy change. This would seem to call for more knowledge and more attentiveness to public affairs than is typical of mass electorates.

But it is crucial that we don't demand that all or even most citizens be knowledgeable. If politics works at the margin, we can observe the aggregate responsiveness of mood if only some citizens are knowledgable and attentive while others are either fixed in place or moving in response to a cacophony of false signals. Like the earlier illustration of elections, movements in national mood are the product of small numbers moving near the middle of the possible range of attitudes.

And the perspective on who moves is helpful. A theory that had committed ideologues changing from left to right or right to left would fail the test of credulity. We expect those who care deeply about the direction of public policy to respond to change in their direction as an appetizer, eager for bigger changes as the main course. Our scorekeepers, however, are anything but committed. Committed to nothing but good outcomes, such as peace and prosperity, their natural response to policy excess is to reverse direction. This should not be understood as an emotional rejection, or a "backlash," but as more mundane, saying in essence, "Okay, we've had a big change in direction. That's enough." They pay enough attention to hear multiple messages that policy has changed, which is the signal readily available in media reports. And when they respond, we see the response as net change in the whole electorate.

Beneath everything in this book is the simple idea that change matters. We have long known that most public opinion most of the time connotes little. People hold opinions about which they do not care and on which they will not act. When opinion changes, however, there has to be some motive force. For that we need to posit citizens who have seen some problem or some government action and formed real views of what should be done about it.

Change becomes a filter through which passes only meaningful responses. The large inert portion of opinion holding, the bandying of words by people who do not care about their content – think of typical citizens being interviewed in a survey – never produces change. It never passes through the filter. The import is that most of the time it just isn't interesting to know what citizens think about topic x. When preferences on x change, then we have a signal that something matters. In this view, opinion dynamics isn't a complement to the study of static public opinion; it is the only thing.

On Symbolic and Operational Ideology

The conflicted conservatives of Chapter 3 don't fit standard accounts of ideology. Recall that just less than a fourth of all Americans profess to think of themselves as "conservative" but express preferences for larger government in numerous domains. They are symbolic conservatives and operational liberals. If "conservative" means conservative, then it can't be squared with support for extension of the scope of government.

To work through this contradiction it is useful to think of our scorekeepers as likely candidates to be conflicted. Unlike the real thing, they can style themselves "conservative" and mean that they are prudent, slow to change, and respect tradition, not knowing that conservatism also entails smaller government and reduced domestic spending. If these people were ideologues, they would buy the whole package. They would be conservative both in symbol and substance or be liberal in both. But people who really have no ideology can nonetheless answer the question of about how they think of themselves, choosing the word "conservative."

What is characteristic of the scorekeepers is focus on outcomes, not programs or policies. They ask about how are things going, not what the government is doing. That frees them to change their views with the times. True conservatives will always oppose expanded government. The scorekeepers are free to call for more spending when it is needed, when, for example, an economic stimulus is needed to speed up lagging economic growth. They can be liberal and Democratic when liberals and Democrats have a good record, or conservative – like their symbolic attachments – and Republican when performance indicators point the other way.

There is a strange contradiction in ideology as a proposed cause of political change. Ideology, in the sense of an elaborate and well-structured world-view, is a wonderful explanation of stability. But structured worldviews are a lifetime thing. Ideology dominates the views of people who never change, and so it can have only a minor role in explaining change. Performance is the opposite. The scorekeepers are asking, "How are you doing?," and responding to the answer.

What we seem to have here is an oxymoron: pragmatic ideologues. How can you be both ideological and pragmatic? If ideology is just identification with the symbol "conservative" and not a commitment to the policy stance of conservatism, then performance issues can dominate politics.

Compare the situations of Ronald Reagan seeking reelection in 1984 and Bill Clinton doing so in 1996. Reagan, the conservative, cut taxes and presided over an improving economy. Clinton, the liberal, raised taxes and also presided over an improved economy. What they have in common is that pragmatists, judging on the factual ground of performance in office, supported both. There is a sense here that ideological change is produced not by true ideologues, who are unvarying in their support for one side, but by people who judge policy by its effects, not its logic.

If it works, it's good. And many professed ideologues end up acting like pragmatists.

On the Horse Race

The presidential campaign polls impress at both ends of the scale. Notably unreliable early in the campaign, they converge reliably to the final result in the last few weeks. That must indicate that those who make their decisions at the key moment – around the party nominating conventions – must constitute a large proportion of all the systematic change of election season.

Again, we have three notably different groups to explain. The committed partisans make their decisions long in advance, many before the campaign begins, before the candidates are known. They contribute to continuity over the campaign, producing no change. They are involved in the primary stage of the campaign, care who becomes the nominee of their party, and follow the progress of events.

The inattentive never tune in. They answer questions when pressed, but their answers signal neither conviction nor intent. Mostly, they will not vote, constituting the great bulk of the eligible electorate that sits out even presidential elections. Some small numbers of them – call them "smart money voters" – will add a little to the winner's margin. Figuring out in the final days which side is projected to win, they care more about voting for a winner – picking the right horse – than they do about what the winner stands for. Or perhaps, knowing nothing else of import, they conclude that likely winners must be somehow better than likely losers and use that little piece of information to make their decisions.[7]

That leaves the horse race to be decided by those of middling interest and knowledge, but no commitment to one side, our scorekeepers. Attentive to outcomes, not party or ideology, they are not involved enough to care much about the early, primary stage of the campaign. They sit on the sideline as judges, watching to see what the parties will do. They are detached, usually having no party and not wishing to involve themselves in producing a candidate.

---

[7] The import of having, say, a percent or so deciding at the last minute to vote for the projected winner is that winners will usually finish stronger than they are projected to do. That is common. Even in cases where it does not provide the winning margin, it is common for winners to beat expectations on election day.

The scorekeepers become involved as judges when the parties begin to present their cases at convention time. Ignoring the hot rhetoric and appeals to the committed, they attend to consensus between the players and commentators on the factual case for having achieved peace and prosperity. When they hear that consensus, they decide. They will vote for the incumbent party if its record is good, for the opposition if not. And these are real decisions. Not like the early soundings, which lack meaning – and therefore accuracy – when the scorekeepers come off the sidelines and make a decision, they are signaling genuine intent. We can see that solidified signal of the last weeks of the presidential race as a replacement phenomenon. People who answer questions without meaning early on are gradually replaced by those indicating real decisions. Those real decisions are not moved by the frantic motions of the final days.

On Response to Government

Partisanship and, to a lesser extent, ideology infuse the political thoughts of most Americans. A Bill Clinton has few Republican admirers, a George W. Bush few Democrats. This is a normal and unremarkable fact of life. We see politics through a prism, of established belief and loyalty. But what is remarkable is that the granting and withdrawing of approval of such figures by the public is almost wholly based on other things and in particular on the quality of performance in office. We see everything through a prism and yet the approval of public figures is based mainly on objective facts. That is a contradiction in need of explanation.

Americans did not become more liberal when they moved from skepticism to growing support for Bill Clinton. What happened, instead, was a reevaluation of the president in line with growing optimism about the domestic economy over the Clinton term. Clearly, Clinton's support was always strong among liberals, opposition always strong among conservatives. To explain change we need to posit the existence of our scorekeepers, people who care about performance and lack the ideological or partisan commitments that would prevent them from changing. Equally clear, the partisan and ideological views that dominate explanation of why some people support and others oppose play almost no role at all in explaining why support moves up and down over time. The aggregate signal carries the movement only of those who move systematically, ignoring the fixed and the random equally.

An event such as the September 11 terrorism changes the perspective somewhat. What is clear in this extraordinary case is that almost all Americans were attentive to the event and responsive to government action. The limit on movement in normal times is that only modest numbers of people are both attentive and uncommitted. The response to all public officials – and the extraordinary response to George W. Bush – show that this proportion of the electorate can grow when something compels the normally inattentive to tune in. Indeed, that suggests an alternative explanation to the rally around the flag phenomenon. The traditional view emphasizes a reevaluation of the president when he speaks for the nation in an international crisis, where people change temporarily from opposition to support. The alternative view is that crisis swells the ranks of those paying attention to government, and the increase comes from those who normally are neither committed nor attentive. That increases the proportion of citizens who drive the signal of response to crisis and president. Neither supporters nor opponents, the normally inattentive become supporters while the president speaks for a united nation in peril. That support necessarily declines over time as crisis wears off and the normally inattentive return to tuning out of government and politics.

ON MARGINAL DEMOCRACY

I wish finally to assess how well democracy works in America. That is difficult, but not less worthy because it is difficult. The word "democracy" is bound up with symbolism, belief, patriotism, and a quasi-religious commitment. It is imbued with our self-identity as Americans. Democracy is the civil religion of America. We so deeply believe in it that it is almost offensive – sacrilegious – to put forward a concrete standard and say, "Let's measure the thing." But that is what I wish to do.

Let me offer a minimal standard of what democracy entails in practice – leaving out lots of associated things, such as freedom, participation, and the dignity of choice. I am interested in assessing the most fundamental meaning of the term, the idea that distinguishes democratic practice from all other forms of governance. That is, I believe, a two-way communication between government and the governed. The essence of democracy in this simple view is that citizens succeed in communicating their preferences to government and that government responds.

This book is about the first of those only, that citizens communicate with government. I have dealt with government response at great length elsewhere with my colleagues Michael MacKuen and Robert Erikson (Erikson et al. 2002). The simple message of that work is that government *does* respond. I'm not going to cover that ground here; I ask the reader just to accept the conclusion.

But everything in this book points to the conclusion that citizens – in the aggregate and at the margin – do succeed in communicating their preferences to government. The evidence shows that they know the drift of public policy and respond in a manner that enforces their (generally moderate) preferences. They hear the message of new issues and new conflicts between the parties and sort themselves over a period to time into the right camps. They attend to the debate of political campaigns and move generally toward the side that has the better factual claim to govern. And equally, they respond to public officials and to government itself, awarding or withholding approval and trust largely again on the basis of factual claims.

Clearly, the "they" here is not all citizens and not even typical citizens. The clear understanding and clear communications arise in the aggregate only because many citizens do not change, and many do not pay enough attention to change sensibly. But because some do succeed in systematically asserting their preferences and because change at the margin is enough to move government, then democracy works.

A democracy in which all citizens weighed equally would be normatively superior to one in which only specialists are carriers of the signal. In democratic theory, one size fits all. But positing uniform citizen behaviors will never produce an accurate descriptive portrait of democracy in America. This working democracy, then, is not a normative ideal.

Do not read into this assertion that government is wise or noble, that it responds efficiently to the demands citizens place on it. We can't know any of those things very well. What we do know is the bare minimum requisite, that its actions produce coherent citizen response and that it responds to that response. That's enough.

Bibliography

Adams, Greg D. 1997. "Abortion: Evidence of Issue Evolution." *American Journal of Political Science* 41:718–37.

Anderson, Jennifer L., and Adam J. Newmark. 2002. "A Dynamic Model of U.S. Senator Approval." *State Politics and Policy Quarterly* 2:298–316.

Brody, Richard A. 1991. *Assessing the President: The Media, Elite Opinion, and Public Support.* Stanford, Calif.: Stanford University Press.

Campbell, Angus, Philip E. Converse, Warren E. Miller, and Donald E. Stokes. 1960. *The American Voter.* New York: Wiley.

Campbell, James E. 2000. *The American Campaign: U.S. Presidential Campaigns and the National Vote.* College Station: Texas A&M University Press.

Carmines, Edward G., and James A. Stimson. 1989. *Issue Evolution: Race and the Transformation of American Politics.* Princeton, N.J.: Princeton University Press.

Conover, Pamela Johnston, and Stanley Feldman. 1981. "The Origins and Meaning of Liberal/Conservative Self-Identifications." *American Journal of Political Science* 25:617–45.

Converse, Philip E. 1964. "The Nature of Belief Systems in Mass Publics." In *Ideology and Discontent,* ed. David E. Apter. Ann Arbor: University of Michigan Press.

Davis, James A., and Tom W. Smith. 1980. "Conservative Weather in a Liberalizing Climate: Change in Selected NORC General Social Survey Items, 1972–1978." *Social Forces* 58:1129–56.

Delli Carpini, Michael X. 1984. "Scooping the Voters? The Consequences of the Networks' Early Call of the 1980 Presidential Race." *Journal of Politics* 46:866–85.

Easton, David. 1965. *A Systems Analysis of Political Life.* New York: Wiley.

Erikson, Robert S., Michael B. MacKuen, and James A. Stimson. 2002. *The Macro Polity.* New York: Cambridge University Press.

Fenno, Richard F. 1978. *Home Style: House Members in Their Districts.* Boston: Little, Brown.

Fiorina, Morris P. 1981. *Retrospective Voting in American National Elections*. New Haven, Conn.: Yale University Press.

Free, Lloyd A., and Hadley Cantril. 1967. *The Political Beliefs of Americans*. New Brunswick, N.J.: Rutgers University Press.

Gelman, Andrew, and Gary King. 1993. "Why Are American Presidential Election Campaign Polls So Variable When Votes Are So Predictable?" *British Journal of Political Science* 23:409–51.

Gilens, Martin. 2000. *Why Americans Hate Welfare*. Chicago: University of Chicago Press.

Hibbing, John R., and Elizabeth Theiss-Morse. 1996. *Congress as Public Enemy*. New York: Cambridge University Press.

Hodrick, R., and E. Prescott. 1980. "Post-War U.S. Business Cycles: An Empirical Investigation." Unpublished paper, Carnegie-Mellon University.

Holbrook, Thomas M. 1996. *Do Campaigns Matter?* Thousand Oaks, Calif.: Sage.

Jackson, John E. 1983. "Election Night Reporting and Voter Turnout." *American Journal of Political Science* 27:615–35.

Keele, Luke. 2002. "Trust in Government as a Macro Concept." Presented at the Annual Meeting of the Midwest Political Science Association, Chicago.

———. 2003. "In Whom Do We Trust?" Ph.D. thesis, University of North Carolina at Chapel Hill.

Kellstedt, Paul M. 2000. "Media Framing and the Dynamics of Racial Policy Preferences." *American Journal of Political Science* 44:245–60.

———. 2003. *The Mass Media and the Dynamics of American Racial Attitudes*. New York: Cambridge University Press.

Kinder, Donald R., and D. Roderick Kiewiet. 1979. "Economic Grievances and Political Behavior: The Role of Personal Discontents and Collective Judgments in Congressional Voting." *American Journal of Political Science* 23:495–527.

Layman, Geoffrey. 2001. *The Great Divide: Religious and Cultural Conflict in American Party Politics*. New York: Columbia University Press.

MacKuen, Michael B., Robert S. Erikson, and James A. Stimson. 1992. "Peasants or Bankers: The American Electorate and the U.S. Economy." *American Political Science Review* 86:597–611.

Mayer, William G. 1992. *The Changing American Mind: How and Why Public Opinion Changed between 1960 and 1988*. Ann Arbor: University of Michigan Press.

———. 2002. "The Swing Voter in American Presidential Elections: A Preliminary Inquiry." Paper prepared for delivery at the Annual Meeting of the American Political Science Association, Boston.

Mueller, John. 1973. *War, Presidents and Public Opinion*. New York: Wiley.

Page, Benjamin I., and Robert Y. Shapiro. 1992. *The Rational Public: Fifty Years of Trends in Americans' Policy Preferences*. Chicago: University of Chicago Press.

Putnam, Robert P. 1995. "Bowling Alone: America's Declining Social Capital." *Journal of Democracy* 6:65–78.

———. 2000. *Bowling Alone*. New York: Simon & Schuster.

Rahn, Wendy M. 2000. "Affect as Information: The Role of Public Mood in Political Reasoning." In *Elements of Reason*, ed. Arthur Lupia, Mathew McCubbins, and Sam Popkins. New York: Cambridge University Press.

Schuman, Howard, Charlotte Steeh, and Lawrence Bobo. 1985. *Racial Attitudes in America: Trends and Interpretations.* Cambridge, Mass.: Harvard University Press.

Smith, Tom W. 1981. "General Liberalism and Social Change in Post World War II America: A Summary of Trends." *Social Indicators Research* 10:1–28.

———. 1987. "That Which We Call Welfare by Any Other Name Would Smell Sweeter: An Analysis of the Impact of Question Wording on Response Patterns." *Public Opinion Quarterly* 51:75–83.

———. 1990. "Liberal and Conservative Trends in the United States since World War II." *Public Opinion Quarterly* 54:479–507.

Stimson, James A. 1991. *Public Opinion in America: Moods, Cycles and Swings.* Boulder, Colo.: Westview.

———. 1998. *Public Opinion in America: Moods, Cycles, and Swings,* 2nd ed. Boulder, Colo.: Westview.

Stokes, Donald E. 1963. "Spatial Models of Party Competition." *American Political Science Review* 57:368–77.

Wlezien, Christopher. 1995. "The Public as Thermostat: Dynamics of Preferences for Spending." *American Journal of Political Science* 39:981–1000.

Wolbrecht, Christina. 2000. *The Politics of Women's Rights: Parties, Positions, and Change.* Princeton, N.J.: Princeton University Press.

Zaller, John R. 1992. *The Nature and Origins of Mass Opinion.* New York: Cambridge University Press.

Zaller, John, and Stanley Feldman. 1992. "A Simple Theory of the Survey Response: Answering Questions and Revealing Preferences." *American Journal of Political Science* 36:579–616.

Index